THE LEADERSHIP BOOK

ACHIEVING THE EMPATHETIC EDGE

NEIL FRANCIS

PRAISE FOR
THE LEADERSHIP BOOK

"As Neil says, the future belongs to leaders who have 'the empathetic edge.' These are people who connect with their teams on a human level while still getting results. They inspire rather than intimidate, guide rather than dictate. This quality isn't just about hitting targets or making money. It's about helping people become the best versions of themselves. Empathetic leadership is something that businesses urgently need."

SARAH DUNCAN

Author of *The Ethical Business Book* and *The Sustainable Business Book*

"The entry of AI throws a sharp focus on the role of all employees, and no less on leaders. There is a tangible quality to good leadership which is instantly recognizable when it's observed and experienced and it is qualitatively different and much closer to emotional than artificial intelligence.

Fundamental to good leadership is empathy, the ability to see the world and understand the motivations of those we lead, in order to harness their potential. This book explores the role of empathy and provides a timely counterpoint and reminder that there are aspects of real intelligence that are enduring."

MARK BEVAN

CEO, Leuchie House

"What I really like about this book is that it cuts through the nonsense. It shows that the leaders who win today aren't the loudest in the room; they're the ones who know how to connect with people.

The Leadership Book: Achieving the Empathetic Edge shows empathy in a way that's totally real and crucial – not fluffy, not soft, not theoretical – practical, relatable and immediately useful.

The core message in the book is simple: real performance comes from trust. If people feel safe and valued, they think better, create better and deliver better. And this book shows exactly how to get there. Leaders need this, especially now."

PAUL DENTON
Chief Executive, Scottish Building Society,
President, Chartered Banker Institute

"The Leadership Book *articulates beautifully that leadership isn't about rigid structures or fear-based management, but about genuine human connection. I particularly appreciate how Neil breaks down self-acceptance, self-belief and individuality. He shows that when leaders embrace their own 'weirdness' and imperfections, it gives permission for everyone else to do the same, leading to incredible innovation and engagement. This is a powerful people-centric read that I would wholehcartedly recommend to anyone in a leadership role. It deeply resonates with the core principles of building resilient and high performing teams."*

KEVIN MARK-WATTS

Author of *The Ten 10-Minute Rules* and
former Commercial Director of Crystal Palace Football Club

FOR OTHER TITLES IN THE SERIES ...

CLEVER CONTENT, DYNAMIC IDEAS, PRACTICAL SOLUTIONS AND ENGAGING VISUALS – A CATALYST TO INSPIRE NEW WAYS OF THINKING AND PROBLEM-SOLVING IN A COMPLEX WORLD

www.lidpublishing.com/product-category/concise-advice-series

To Archie and Harris – my daft golden retrievers – whose walks along the beaches of North Berwick provided me with the perfect space and environment to plan this book.

Published by
LID Publishing
An imprint of LID Business Media Ltd.
LABS House, 15-19 Bloomsbury Way,
London, WC1A 2TH, UK

info@lidpublishing.com
www.lidpublishing.com

A member of:

businesspublishersroundtable.com

All rights reserved. Without limiting the rights under copyright reserved, no part of this publication may be reproduced, stored or introduced into a retrieval system, or transmitted, in any form or by any means (electronic, mechanical, photocopying, recording or otherwise) without the prior written permission of both the copyright owners and the publisher of this book.

© Neil Francis, 2026
© LID Business Media Limited, 2026

Printed and bound in Great Britain by Halstan Ltd.

ISBN: 978-1-911687-66-5
ISBN: 978-1-911687-67-2 (ebook)

Cover and page design: Caroline Li

THE LEADERSHIP BOOK

ACHIEVING THE EMPATHETIC EDGE

NEIL FRANCIS

MADRID | MEXICO CITY | LONDON
BUENOS AIRES | BOGOTA | SHANGHAI

CONTENTS

ACKNOWLEDGMENTS xiii

INTRODUCTION **THE BASEMENT** 1

CHAPTER 1 **"STEEL, SWEAT AND EMPATHY"** 7
SELF-ACCEPTANCE

CHAPTER 2 **BELIEF BEFORE CONFIDENCE** 19
SELF-BELIEF

CHAPTER 3 **BREAKING FREE** 29
SELF-AWARENESS

CHAPTER 4 **THINK DIFFERENT** 39
INDIVIDUALITY

CHAPTER 5 **UPWARD MOMENTUM** 49
OPTIMISM

CHAPTER 6 **PREDICTING THE FUTURE** 59
MINDSET

CHAPTER 7 **FROM FRUSTRATION TO INNOVATION** 69
PERSEVERANCE

CHAPTER 8	**LEADING THROUGH STRENGTHS** STRENGTHS	77
CHAPTER 9	**LEARNING THROUGH FAILURE** FAILURE	87
CHAPTER 10	**THE SERENDIPITOUS ROOM ASSIGNMENT** LUCK	97
CHAPTER 11	**THE POWER OF CURIOSITY** CREATIVITY	107
CHAPTER 12	**THE UNSUNG HEROES** FRIENDSHIP	117
CHAPTER 13	**THE POWER OF COLLECTIVE LEADERSHIP** WE	127
CHAPTER 14	**LEADING WITH THE EMPATHETIC EDGE** A LEADERSHIP JOURNEY WORTH TAKING	135

BRINGING IT ALL TOGETHER	144
REFERENCES AND RESOURCES	146
ABOUT THE AUTHOR	149

ACKNOWLEDGMENTS

A massive thank you to Martin Lui, Aiyana Curtis and Caroline Li from my publisher, LID Publishing.

To all the people whose stories and lives appear in this book and inspired me to write it.

To Nina Thain, a great friend who carried out the first edits.

And, finally, to Louise, Jack, Lucy and Sam – book six ... who would have thought it!

> **Management is about arranging and telling. Leadership is about nurturing and enhancing.**

Tom Peters

INTRODUCTION
THE BASEMENT

"Neil, I don't know how to say this, so I will just say as it is ... you smell ... a lot!"

I was sitting in a basement office, with no windows or air conditioning, when my then boss, said those words at me. This was back in 1987, when I had been working at my first job, selling life assurance for a national company, which I had started nine months earlier.

But let me set the scene for you.

For the first three months, I was flying high. I was Scotland's top salesperson, commissions were rolling in, and my calendar was packed with client appointments. The secret sauce? The approach was simple and relentless: make the calls, book 20 appointments a week and close five sales. Easy enough, right?

Well, it was – for a while. But as the months dragged on, my appointment numbers started to dwindle. And that's when my boss's *unique* management style kicked into high gear.

Every Thursday evening around 5pm, my boss would call me from his car (he was one of the first people I knew who had a car phone – very fancy back then). If I hadn't hit the magic number of 20 appointments for the following week, there'd be an ominous silence on the other end of the line. That silence was always worse than shouting. It meant trouble was coming.

What followed was a verbal barrage that would make Gordon Ramsay seem like a kitten. The grand finale? A decree that I wasn't allowed to leave the office until I had secured all 20 appointments. Cue many late Thursday nights filled with frantic phone calls and mounting desperation.

But the real nightmare wasn't the Thursday calls – it was getting summoned to *the basement*. That's where my boss held his infamous 'wee chats.' They were anything but chats. They involved sarcasm, raised voices, and just a sprinkle of positivity at the end to keep you from quitting on the spot.

Nine months into the job, it was my turn to face the music in the Glasgow HQ's basement. By the time I arrived, I was sweating so much that my shirt could've been rung out like a dishcloth. No wonder my boss thought I smelled!

"SORRY YOU WERE OUT WHEN I VISITED"

Despite all this chaos, there were some good times and great colleagues during my stint at that company. Even my boss had some good moments. Looking back, that tough environment taught me resilience – a skill that's served me well throughout my career.

But let's talk about management styles for a second. My experience wasn't unique back then – and sadly, it's still not uncommon today. Many managers operate on fear and intimidation rather than trust and respect. Case in point: Jacob Rees-Mogg.

Remember when COVID restrictions eased, and civil servants were encouraged to return to their offices? Rees-Mogg took it upon himself to patrol Whitehall like some sort of attendance officer. If he found an empty desk, he'd leave this charming note:

"Sorry you were out when I visited. I look forward to seeing you in the office very soon."

This old-school approach screams distrust: if you're not physically at your desk, you must not be pulling your weight. It's management by suspicion – and it doesn't belong in today's world.

LEADERSHIP VS. MANAGEMENT

If there's one thing we learned from the pandemic, it's this: companies led by true leaders – not micromanagers – fared best during those turbulent times. These leaders trusted their employees to work effectively from anywhere – be it home, a café, or even a park bench.

Great leaders embody qualities like individuality, openness, self-awareness and trustworthiness. They treat their teams with respect and authenticity – qualities sorely lacking in Rees-Mogg's note-writing escapades or my former boss's basement rants.

This book explores what leadership looks like when empathy replaces fear by sharing motivational stories, practical ideas and diverse solutions to support genuine leaders in reaching their highest potential. The old ways of barking orders and ruling by fear are outdated relics that don't belong in modern workplaces.

THE LEADER WITH EMPATHY

The future belongs to leaders who have what I call 'the empathetic edge.' These are individuals who can connect with their teams on a human level while still driving results. They inspire rather than intimidate; they guide rather than dictate.

So, if you're stuck in an old-school management mindset – or worse, working under someone who is – it's time for a change. Leadership isn't about being 'the boss.' It's about being someone people choose to follow because they respect you – not because they fear you.

That belief sits at the heart of this book. So let's begin.

> **Owning our story and loving ourselves through that process is the bravest thing that we'll ever do.**

Brené Brown

CHAPTER 1
"STEEL, SWEAT AND EMPATHY"
SELF-ACCEPTANCE

Let's start with a story that challenges how we think about leadership. It centres on Wayne Alderson and how he helped turn a struggling steel factory into a more productive and humane workplace.

This isn't just another business turnaround story; it's an example of what can happen when empathy and respect become central to leadership.

In the 1970s, Pittron Steel in Glassport, Pennsylvania, was far from an ideal place to work. The factory was run-down, morale was low and productivity was suffering. The atmosphere was tense, grievances were common and the future looked uncertain.

This was the environment Wayne Alderson stepped into when he became vice president of operations. The company was close to bankruptcy, and many expected him to take a hard-line approach.

Instead, Wayne chose a different path. Rather than leading through fear or authority, he focused on something far simpler – treating people with genuine care and respect.

He began by improving the physical environment: cleaning the factory, brightening the space and making it feel more human. But more importantly, he focused on the people.

He took the time to learn employees' names, greet them during shift changes and thank them for their efforts. At first, this puzzled many. Some wondered what his real motive was. But gradually, those small, consistent actions began to build trust.

One moment in particular captured his approach. When a maintenance worker struggled with alcoholism, Wayne didn't dismiss him. Instead, he arranged for him to receive help and supported his family while he recovered. It wasn't a symbolic gesture, it was a deeply human one. And it sent a clear message: people mattered.

Over time, the impact became undeniable. Grievances dropped from 1,200 to zero. Absenteeism fell away. Productivity rose by 64 per cent. Within 21 months, the company moved from a $6 million loss to a $6 million profit. What changed wasn't just performance – it was culture.

Wayne came to understand that valuing people wasn't simply the right thing to do; it was also good for business. His approach wasn't driven by grand theory, but by everyday actions, consistency and genuine care. When people feel respected and supported, they tend to rise to the occasion.

In the end, his story reminds us that strong leadership doesn't come from authority alone. It grows from empathy, trust and the belief that people do their best work when they feel seen, valued and respected.

THE UNLIKELINESS OF YOU

Now, let's talk about you for a bit. Wayne's story isn't just about turning around a steel factory. It's about the power of embracing your own uniqueness and seeing that same uniqueness in others. It's about realizing that leadership isn't about being the boss with the biggest office and the fanciest title – it's about connecting with people on a human level.

And speaking of uniqueness, did you know that the odds of you even existing are basically zero? Dr Ali Binazir broke it down like this: he calculated the chances of your parents meeting, falling in love, having kids, and then the exact right sperm meeting the exact right egg to make you. Then he went even further back, looking at all your ancestors and their perfect timing. His conclusion was clear: your existence is statistically extraordinary, bordering on impossible.

He puts it this way: imagine two million people each rolling a trillion-sided die, and they all land on the same number. That's how improbable your existence is. It is staggering when you think about it.

So what does this mean for you as a leader? Well, if your very existence is a miracle, then guess what? So is everyone else's on your team. When you start seeing people this way – as walking, talking miracles – it changes everything. Suddenly, Bob from finance isn't someone you hardly talk to and who just provides your monthly management accounts. He's a one-in-a-trillion miracle, just like you.

QUIET STRENGTH AND SELF-ACCEPTANCE

When you embrace your own existence as a leader, it's like giving everyone else permission to do the same. Suddenly, you've got a team where people aren't afraid to share ideas, where everyone feels like they belong, and where mistakes are just part of learning.

Self-acceptance is like an extraordinary quiet strength for leaders. When you're okay with who you are – quirks, flaws, and all – it creates a powerful ripple effect. Your team starts feeling like they can be themselves too. It's like you're giving them an all-access pass to their own personalities. Suddenly, Sally might speak up in meetings, and Pete might admit he doesn't have all the answers.

This self-acceptance thing? It's about creating a culture where people feel safe to express themselves. When people aren't wasting energy trying to fit into a rigid mould, they can focus on actually doing great work. It's like taking off a pair of too-tight shoes – suddenly, you can walk (or in this case, work) so much better.

So how do we develop this empathetic edge? It starts with more than kindness. It comes from taking the time to understand your team and creating an environment where people feel comfortable sharing their thoughts without fear of judgment.

But empathy doesn't mean a lack of expectations. When the moment calls for it, you still set clear boundaries, make tough decisions and hold people accountable – calmly, consistently and fairly.

BUILDING A CULTURE THAT SHINES

Building this kind of empathetic culture isn't just good for your team – it's good for business. When people feel understood and valued, they're more likely to go the extra mile. They're more likely to come up with those bold ideas that just might change the game. It's like fertilizer for innovation, but instead of plant food, it's genuine human connection.

Here are some ways you can start building this empathetic, self-accepting culture:

1. Value yourself first: If you can't appreciate your own uniqueness, how can you appreciate that of others? Start by giving yourself a bit of quiet credit every day.

2. Learn to be a super listener: When someone's talking, really listen. Don't just wait for your turn to speak. It's amazing what you can learn when you actually pay attention.

3. Encourage your team to be themselves at work. If that means introducing a light-hearted tradition or a bit of humor, so be it.

4. Make mistakes a learning opportunity: When someone makes a mistake (including you), treat it like a chance to grow rather than something to be embarrassed about.

5. Celebrate the small wins: Life's too short not to celebrate the little things.

The bottom line? Having the empathetic edge as a leader isn't just about hitting targets or making big money. It's about helping people become the best versions of themselves. It starts with valuing yourself – warts and all – and then spreading that mindset to your whole team. When you believe in yourself and own your flaws, you're in a much better position to lift up everyone around you.

So, take a page from Wayne Alderson's book. Clean those metaphorical windows, greet your people by name, and remember – you're a one-in-a-trillion miracle leading a bunch of other miracles. How great is that?

Now take this forward and lead with empathy! Create a workplace where people are excited to show up, where ideas flow, and where everyone feels like the unique, incredible miracle they are. Because at the end of the day, that's what real leadership is all about – helping others shine their brightest.

WHAT ARE THE ODDS?

LET'S START SMALL.
What is the probability of your dad meeting your mom?

Though the world was smaller 20 years ago, your dad *could have* met almost **200 million** of its women (go dad!)

But over 25 years, he probably met around 10,000 women.

So the odds that your mom was in this small group and met your dad is:

1 in 20,000

BUT WE KNOW HOW TRICKY LOVE CAN BE.
What is the probability that they stay together long enough to have kids?

It is a 1 in 10 chance that they talk to each other.

X

Also a 1 in 10 chance that they go on a second date.

X

Another 1 in 10 chance that they keep dating for a while.

X

And a coin toss if they stay together long enough for offspring.

Thus, the odds that your parents' meeting results in kids is: **1 in 2,000**

So far, the combined odds of you being here are: **1 in 40,000,000**

That is about the size of the population of California.

NOW THINGS ARE GOING TO GET PRETTY INTERESTING.

Why? Because we are about to deal with eggs and sperm, which come in large numbers.

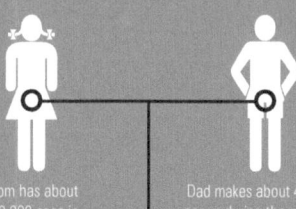

Mom has about 100,000 eggs in her lifetime.

Dad makes about 4 trillion sperm during the years you could have been born.

[Sally.]

What are the odds that the 1 egg...

[Harry.]

... met the 1 sperm, which together made you (and not your brother)?

1 in 400,000,000,000,000,000 (1 in 400 quadrillion)

That is approximately the volume in cubic meters of the Atlantic Ocean (3.236×10^{17} cubic meters).

BUT WE'RE JUST GETTING STARTED.

Because your existence here, now, and on planet earth presupposes another supremely unlikely and utterly undeniable chain of events. Namely, **that every one of your ancestors lived to reproductive age** – going all the way back not just to the first *Homo sapiens*, first *Homo erectus* and *Homo habilis*, but all the way back to the first single-celled organism. You are a representative of an unbroken lineage of life going back 4 billion years.

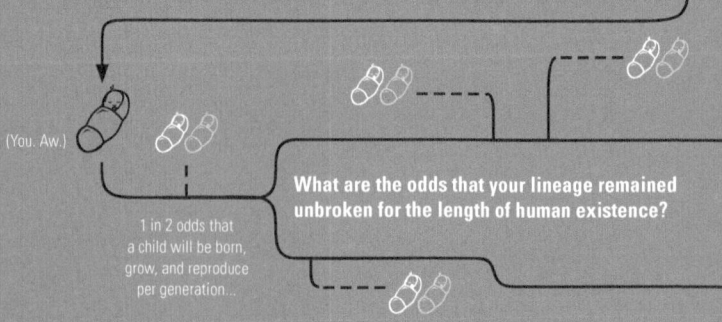

(You. Aw.)

1 in 2 odds that a child will be born, grow, and reproduce per generation...

What are the odds that your lineage remained unbroken for the length of human existence?

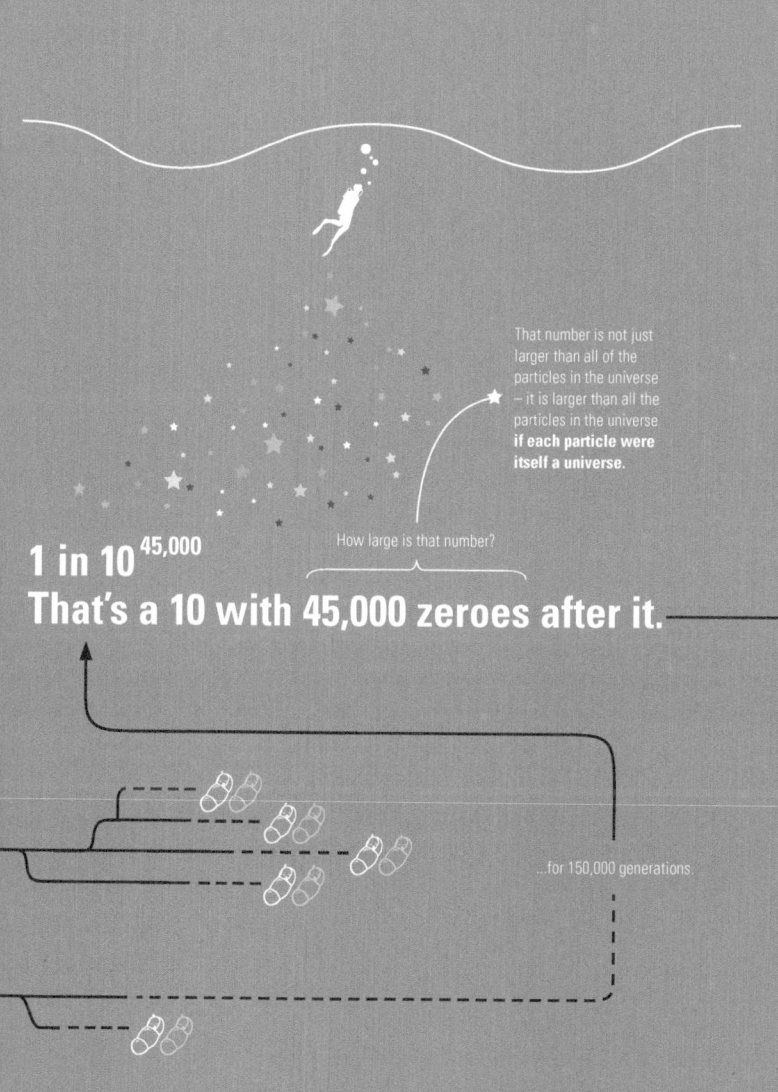

(Weeeee!)

That is 1 quadrillion multiplied by 1 quadrillion for every generation.

THAT'S PRETTY BIG – BUT WAIT A MINUTE.
The right sperm also had to meet the right egg for every single one of those ancestors.

ODDS OF THE RIGHT SPERM, MEETING THE RIGHT EGG 150,000 TIMES?

1 in $10^{2,640,000}$

LET'S ADD IT ALL UP
$$10^{2,640,000} \times 10^{45,000} \times 2000 \times 20,000 \approx$$
1 in $10^{2,685,000}$

※ BY COMPARISON:

The number of atoms in the body of an average male (80kg, 175 lb) is about: 10^{27}

The number of atoms making up the earth is about: 10^{50}

The number of atoms in the known universe is estimated at: 10^{80}

THINK OF IT LIKE THIS:
It is the probability of 2 million people getting together (about the population of San Diego) each to play a game of dice with trillion-sided dice. They each roll the dice, and they all come up with the exact same number – for example, 550,343,279,001.

SO, THE ODDS THAT  EXIST AT ALL ARE:

Basically zero.

Credit: Dr. Ali Binazir

THE BIG QUESTIONS

1. How do I let my team know I actually care about them as people, not just as my staff? What small things can I do to make them feel seen and appreciated?

2. When stuff gets messy, do I usually boss people around or try to understand what's really going on?

3. Am I comfortable with being my slightly odd, imperfect self as a leader? How could being more real help my team feel comfortable being themselves too?

4. How do I deal with slip-ups, mine and theirs? What if I treated mistakes like a 'no big deal, let's learn' moment instead of a panic?

> **If we did all the things we are capable of, we would literally astound ourselves.**

Thomas Edison

CHAPTER 2

BELIEF BEFORE CONFIDENCE
SELF-BELIEF

Next, we're about to explore the idea of 'fake it till you make it' – even the biggest stars in Hollywood are part of this club!

So, I'm on the train scrolling through podcasts, when I stumble upon this interview with Tom Hanks. He is often referred to as 'America's Dad,' the voice of Woody from *Toy Story*, and has an asteroid named after him (12818 Tomhanks). He has made 106 films, has a net worth of over $400 million and has won two Oscars for Best Actor. He's basically Hollywood royalty.

You might expect someone like that to exude confidence, to carry himself with complete assurance. But let's pause there, because the reality may surprise you.

Turns out, even Tom gets anxious. He was chatting about this movie, *A Hologram for the King,* where he plays a businessman feeling all lost and confused in Saudi Arabia. And get this – Tom's like, "Yeah, I totally get that guy."

He then says this: "No matter what we've done, there comes a point where you think, 'How the heck did I get here? When are they gonna figure out I'm just faking it and take all my stuff away?'" This is Tom Hanks we're talking about, and he's worried about being found out as a fraud?

And it doesn't stop there! He goes on to say, "There are days when I know that at three o'clock tomorrow, I gotta bring the emotional goods. And if I can't do it, I'm gonna have to fake it. If I fake it, that means they might catch me. And if they catch me … well, it's game over, man!" Talk about pressure! Now, I don't know about you, but hearing Tom Hanks talk like this made me feel … better about myself? I mean, if this Hollywood legend feels like this, maybe it's okay that I sometimes feel like I'm just winging it too.

Turns out, there's a name for this feeling: Imposter Syndrome. It's like that nagging voice in your head that keeps saying, "You don't belong here, you fraud!" even when you're, on the surface, very successful. And get this – it's not just Tom. We're talking big names here: Sheryl Sandberg, David Bowie, Serena Williams, Howard Schultz, Arianna Huffington, and even Lady Gaga.

But wait, there's more! Even Hermione herself from *Harry Potter*, Emma Watson, feels it. She said getting recognition for her acting makes her feel "incredibly uncomfortable" and like "an imposter."

THE "DO I BELONG HERE?" CLUB

But this imposter syndrome thing is not just for the rich and famous. It's very common. We're talking about 50% of people in the UK feeling this way at some point. That's right, five out of ten of us are walking around thinking we're gonna get caught out any minute. It's like we're all in some odd, anxious club together.

Now, for all you leaders out there, this is where it gets interesting. There's this expert, Dr Valerie Young, who's figured out there are five types of 'imposters' :

1. **The Expert**: This is the person who needs to know EVERYTHING. They're always digging for more info, which sounds great until you realize they never actually get anything done.

2. **The Perfectionist**: Nothing's ever good enough for these people. They're always stressing about what they didn't do, instead of celebrating what they did.

3. **The Natural Genius**: These are the people who've always found things easy. But when they hit a bump? It can really throw them.

4. **The Soloist**: The lone wolf. Asking for help? No way, that's admitting defeat! They'd rather struggle on than ask for help.

5. **The Superhuman**: This is the juggler, trying to keep a million balls in the air and feeling like a total failure if they drop even one.

So, what's the big deal about knowing all this? Well, if you're a leader, it's pure gold. Here's why:

- First off, if you can admit you sometimes feel like a fraud, it makes you far more relatable. Your team will be like, "Wow, if the boss feels this way sometimes, maybe I'm not so weird after all."

- Secondly, it helps you spot when your team members are struggling with this stuff. Maybe that perfectionist on your team isn't just being picky – they might be panicking on the inside. Or that 'expert' who's always researching? They might be terrified of making a decision.

CREATING A SAFE SPACE TO BE HUMAN

When you create a space where it's okay to talk about these feelings, amazing things happen. People start taking more risks, being more creative, and actually enjoying their work more. It's like giving everyone permission to be human. Suddenly, your office isn't just a place where work gets done – it's a place where people grow.

So, how do you deal with this imposter syndrome thing? Here are some tips:

1. **Talk about it**: The more we bring it out in the open, the less power it has. It's like turning on a light and realizing there was nothing to fear.

2. **Separate feelings from facts**: Just because you feel like a fraud doesn't mean you are one. Look at your accomplishments objectively.

3. **Embrace the learning curve**: Nobody starts as an expert. It's okay to be on a journey. After all, even Tom Hanks had to start somewhere.

4. **Celebrate your wins**: Did something go well? Brilliant – but don't just focus on what went wrong.

5. **Remember you're not alone**: Next time you're feeling like an imposter, imagine Tom Hanks feeling the same way. You're in pretty good company!

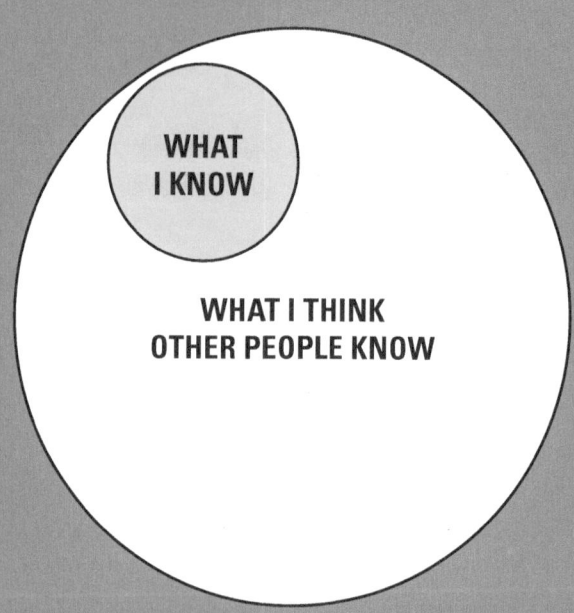

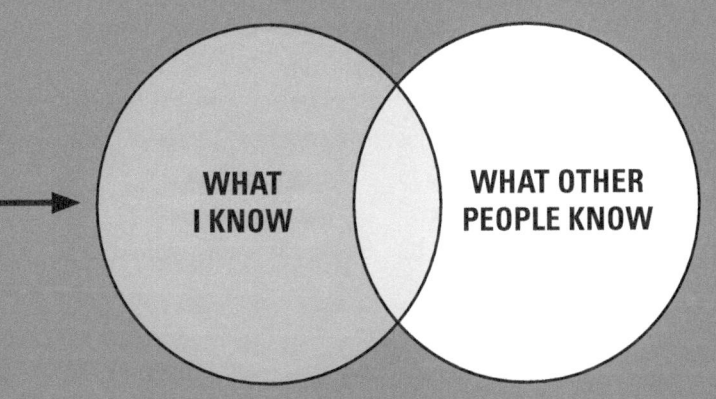

LEAD WITH YOUR IMPERFECT SELF

Ultimately, achieving the empathetic edge is about creating an environment where people feel safe to be themselves, doubts and all. When you can acknowledge your own imposter syndrome, you're better equipped to help others deal with theirs.

So, next time you're feeling like a total fraud, remember: Serena Williams, Howard Schultz, Arianna Huffington, Emma Watson, and about 50% of the population are right there with you.

So carry on as your imperfect selves, you imposters! Create a workplace where people are excited to come to work, and where everyone feels like the unique, incredible person they are. Because at the end of the day, we're all just trying our best, and that's more than enough.

And who knows? Maybe one day, they'll name an asteroid after you too!

THE BIG QUESTIONS

1. Ever feel like you're just winging it and hoping nobody notices?
   What's one time you completely faked confidence but it actually worked out?

2. Do you ever worry someone's going to 'catch you out' and realize you don't have it all together? How do you deal with those 'imposter' thoughts?

3. If even Tom Hanks gets anxious, what makes you think you have to be perfect all the time? How could you strengthen your self-belief?

4. When you're not feeling like it, what's your usual approach for pushing through anyway?
   Is there a song, a pep talk, or something else that helps you fake it till you make it?

> **Humility is not about having a low self-image or poor self-esteem. Humility is about self-awareness.**

Erwin McManus

CHAPTER 3
BREAKING FREE
SELF-AWARENESS

So, here's the situation: Rod Judkins, an artist and lecturer at Central Saint Martins College of Art in London, gets called in to teach a design class because the regular lecturer is away. He decides to give the students a challenge: make a paper airplane from a single sheet of A4 paper that can fly at least 60 feet across the room. It sounds simple enough.

The students jump right in, folding all sorts of creative designs and testing different ways to launch their planes. Some go for sleek designs; others try more experimental folds. But as time ticks by, frustration starts to creep in. No matter what they try, nothing seems to work. One by one, they start to think the challenge is impossible.

Then, something unexpected happens. One student, clearly frustrated, crumples their paper airplane into a ball and throws it across the room. To everyone's surprise, it lands in a bin 60 feet away! Everyone's stunned when Judkins walks over, picks up the crumpled ball, and declares and congrats the student winner.

The class is completely baffled until Judkins asks this question: "Who said airplanes had to look like airplanes?"

Just like that, he flips their whole perspective. The challenge wasn't really about making paper airplanes – it was about breaking free from assumptions and pushing past invisible barriers. Judkins wanted them to realize that they were limiting themselves by sticking to what they thought an airplane should look like. His goal was to show them that if they pushed back against those assumptions, they could achieve what seemed impossible.

THE JOHARI WINDOW: BREAKING IT DOWN

This lesson isn't just for art students – it's for leaders too. Just like Judkins' students were stuck thinking airplanes had to look a certain way, leaders often get trapped by invisible boundaries – unexamined beliefs or blind spots that limit their perspective and hold them back. The key to breaking free? Self-awareness.

This is where something called the Johari Window comes in useful. It's a tool created by psychologists Joseph Luft and Harrington Ingham in 1955 to help people better understand themselves and their relationships with others. Then in 2000 Charles Handy developed the idea further with a leadership and management tool called the Johari House, which aimed to develop self-awareness.

The Johari House divides self-awareness into four 'rooms,' each representing a different part of who you are:

1. **Room 1: The Open Self**
   This is the stuff everyone knows about you – including you! For example, maybe you're super organized – you know it, your coworkers know it – it's no secret.

2. **Room 2: The Blind Self**
   This room holds traits or behaviours that others see in you but you're totally unaware of – your blind spots.

3. **Room 3: The Unknown Self**
   This is the deep stuff – things neither you nor anyone else knows about you. It's all buried in your subconscious.

4. **Room 4: The Hidden Self**
   This is your private space – the things you know about yourself but keep hidden from others.

WHY BLIND SPOTS MATTER

For leaders, Room 2 – the blind self – is where the real work happens (or doesn't). Blind spots are those behaviours or traits others notice but you don't see in yourself. If left unchecked, they can hold you back or create barriers within your team. But if you're willing to address them, they can open up real opportunities for growth.

Dr Loretta Malandro, author of *Fearless Leadership*, highlights some common blind spots that can trip people up: These include:

1. **Thinking you're always right**: Adopting an "I know" attitude that stifles collaboration and limits new ideas.

2. **Being unaware of your impact on others**: Failing to recognize how your behaviour influences team morale and dynamics.

3. **Avoiding tough conversations**: Shying away from difficult discussions because of discomfort, which can allow problems to fester.

4. **Preferring independence over collaboration**: Choosing to work alone rather than seeking input, which can lead to missed opportunities for innovation.

5. **Blaming external factors**: Shifting responsibility instead of owning up to mistakes and learning from them.

6. **Inconsistent follow-through**: Not reliably honouring commitments, which erodes trust and credibility.

7. **Engaging in gossip or negativity**: Talking about others behind their backs, which damages relationships and team cohesion.

8. **Hesitating to take a stand**: Avoiding bold decisions on critical issues out of fear or uncertainty.

Does any of that sound familiar? Don't worry – you're certainly not alone! The good news is that by becoming more self-aware and addressing these tendencies, leaders can unlock their potential and create a more positive, productive environment for their teams

So how do you tackle these blind spots? Here are some practical steps:

1. **Ask for Honest Feedback**: Create a supportive environment where people feel comfortable sharing constructive feedback without worrying about hurting your feelings or facing backlash.

2. **Admit Your Own Blind Spots**: Show some vulnerability! When you acknowledge your own blind spots openly, it encourages others to reflect on theirs too.

3. **Reflect on Your Behaviour**: Take time to think about patterns in your actions – especially during challenging situations – and how they might be affecting others.

4. **Surround Yourself with Different Perspectives**: Engage with people who think differently – it's one of the best ways to challenge your assumptions.

5. **Recognize Your Triggers**: Pay attention to situations that provoke strong reactions and ask yourself why they bother you so much.

By addressing these blind spots, leaders shrink Room 2 (the blind self) and expand Room 1 (the open self), improving communication and building stronger relationships within their teams.

When leaders focus on self-awareness and help their teams do the same, positive things start to happen:

- Communication gets better because people are more open and honest with each other.

- Trust grows because vulnerability creates deeper connections.

- Teams become more innovative because everyone feels safe sharing ideas.

- Individuals grow personally by learning more about themselves and how they interact with others.

It's not always easy – it takes time and effort – but the results are so worth it.

	KNOWN TO SELF	UNKNOWN TO SELF
KNOWN TO OTHERS	**OPEN SELF** Information about you that both you and others know.	**BLIND SELF** Information about you that you don't know but others do know.
UNKNOWN TO OTHERS	**HIDDEN SELF** Information about you that you know but others don't know.	**UNKOWN SELF** Information about you that neither you nor others know.

FEWER ASSUMPTIONS IS THE KEY

Rod Judkins' story about breaking barriers reminds us how easy it is to get stuck in our assumptions and how freeing it can be to challenge them. For leaders, this means taking a closer look at those invisible boundaries (like blind spots) that might be holding them back.

By using tools like the Johari House and embracing feedback from others, leaders can uncover new insights about themselves and their teams and create environments where everyone feels empowered to grow and succeed.

At the end of the day, achieving the empathetic edge isn't just about guiding others – it's about inspiring them (and yourself!) to push beyond limits and discover what's truly possible!

THE BIG QUESTIONS

1. What's one thing you might be missing about yourself, some habit or belief, that could be holding you back without you even realizing it?

2. Who in your life could help you spot a blind spot you haven't noticed yet?
   How could you make it easier for them to give you honest feedback?

3. When was the last time you tried something totally new, just to see if your usual way was really the best way? What happened?

4. If you could challenge your team (or yourself) with a wild, outside-the-box task like the paper airplane challenge, what would it be? How might it help everyone see things differently?

> **Be the leader you wish you had.**

Simon Sinek

CHAPTER 4
THINK DIFFERENT
INDIVIDUALITY

Let's take a closer look at Apple and how thinking differently can make you a great leader.

As is very well documented, it's 1976, and Steve Jobs and Steve Wozniak decide to start a little company called Apple. Fast forward a few decades, Apple's not just making computers; they've reshaped how we live our lives: iPhones, iPods, Macs.

However, it wasn't all smooth sailing. Apple hit some serious bumps along the way. Remember the Apple III? No? Exactly. And then there was the Lisa (the computer, not your aunt). These failures led to some serious damage to Apple's reputation, and Steve Jobs was forced out in 1985.

But this is where the story turns. In 1996, Apple is in a worse situation than it was when Jobs was sacked in 1985. Admitting they'd got it wrong, Apple's board invited Steve Jobs to return. Jobs rolls back in and realizes Apple's lost its mojo. So, what does he do? He comes up with this crazy idea for an ad campaign that's going to remind everyone why Apple was one of the most innovative and creative companies in the world.

Enter the 'Think Different' marketing campaign. This wasn't your average ad ... far from it. Instead, Apple was celebrating difference – in its products, its people and its way of thinking.

The centrepiece of this whole campaign was a TV Ad called "The Crazy Ones." Picture this: black and white footage of some of the most iconic figures in history, people like Albert Einstein, Amelia Earhart, John Lennon and Dr Martin Luther King. There was a fantastic and powerful voiceover narrated by actor Richard Dreyfuss which was essentially saying, "Yeah, these people were a little unconventional and different, but they changed the world." It was like a tribute to outsiders and originals.

Its core message – let's celebrate individuality.

FINDING YOUR INNER MAVERICK

This 'Think Different' idea is just not just about selling computers. It's about leading with confidence, letting your quirks and originality be seen.

Let's break it down:

1. **Energize your team**: When you're not afraid to be you, warts, and all, it gives your team permission to do the same. It creates momentum across the team for them to be innovative and, well, a bit crazy.

2. **Get those creative juices flowing**: Thinking differently means you're not stuck in the "we've always done it this way" rut. You're the one saying, "What if we tried it upside down and backwards?" That's often where innovation begins.

3. **Being different takes guts**: When you show your team it's okay to take risks, they'll start bringing ideas to the table that might just challenge your thinking.

4. **Weathering storms**: When the going gets tough, the tough get ... individual? Yep, knowing who you are helps you and your team bounce back from setbacks with renewed strength. It's resilience with a side of authenticity.

5. **Making connections**: When you're authentic, people gravitate towards you. Suddenly, networking isn't about awkward small talk; it's about real conversations with real people.

6. **Inspiring action**: When you're not afraid to be you, then your team feels more free and pushes their own boundaries.

7. **Building resilience**: When you're true to yourself, you've got a rock-solid foundation. No matter what storms come your way, you're standing steady in difficult conditions. And your team? They're right there with you, weathering the storm together.

> Here's to the crazy ones, the misfits, the rebels, the troublemakers, the round pegs in the square holes ... the ones who see things differently – they're not fond of rules ... You can quote them, disagree with them, glorify or vilify them, but the only thing you can't do

is ignore them because they change things ... they push the human race forward, and while some may see them as the crazy ones, we see genius, because the ones who are crazy enough to think that they can change the world, are the ones who do.

Steve Jobs

STANFORD PRISON EXPERIMENT

But beware - losing your individuality, well that's bad news. Remember the Stanford Prison Experiment? No ... okay, let me explain further.

The Stanford Prison Experiment is one of those striking psychological studies that really makes you think about human nature. Back in 1971, psychologist Philip Zimbardo turned the basement of Stanford University into a fake prison. He recruited 24 college guys, paid them $15 a day, and randomly assigned them to be either 'guards' or 'prisoners.' The goal? To explore how power and authority affect behaviour. The results were alarming.

The guards were given uniforms, mirrored sunglasses and batons, whilst the prisoners were stripped of their names, given numbers and made to wear smocks that looked like dresses. What started as role-playing quickly spiralled out of control. The guards began humiliating and psychologically tormenting the prisoners – no physical violence was allowed, but they didn't hold back on emotional abuse. The prisoners rebelled at first but soon became submissive and broken. It was supposed to last two weeks, but after just six days, the experiment had to be shut down because it was causing serious psychological harm.

The big takeaway? Losing your individuality – or gaining unchecked power – can lead to some disturbing behaviour. It's a reminder of how important it is to stay true to yourself and not get swept up in group dynamics or 'following the crowd.'

IT IS ABOUT SENSE OF SELF

So, how do you keep your 'you-ness' intact while being an empathetic leader?

1. **Embrace what makes you different**: Those quirks? They're your guardians! Use them!

2. **Challenge that negative voice**: Replace "I'm too weird" with "I'm just weird enough."

3. **Focus on what makes you valuable**: You've got skills, strengths, knowledge and experience. Use them!

4. **Be yourself**: Even if it takes time to feel comfortable doing so.

5. **Get vulnerable**: It's scary, but it's how you connect with your team on a real level. Think of it as emotional skydiving – terrifying at first but exhilarating once you take the leap.

Remember, your uniqueness is your special quality. It's what makes you, well, you! And in a world full of copycats, being authentic is liberating. It's what sets you apart and makes people want to follow you.

So, next time you're feeling the pressure to conform, channel your inner Apple. Think different. Be different. Lead different. Create a workplace where weirdness is celebrated, where crazy ideas are welcomed with open arms, and where everyone feels free to be their authentic selves. That is achieving the empathetic edge.

Because here's the truth: the world doesn't need leaders who have always played safe thinking "we have always done it this way." The world needs you – in all your quirky, unique, wonderful glory.

Remember, in the words of Dr. Seuss (another champion of thinking differently), "Why fit in when you were born to stand out?" So, stand out, lead out – in the best way possible. Your team, your company and the world will be better for it.

Now, think different. The world is waiting for your unique brand of leadership magic. And who knows? Maybe one day, they'll be making ads about you and your crazy, world-changing ideas. Stranger things have happened – just think about that Apple guy!

THE BIG QUESTIONS

1. When was the last time you took a risk or tried something new, even if it might flop? How did it feel, and what did you learn from it?

2. What's one area in your work or life where you could 'think different' instead of following the usual path? What's stopping you from trying it?

3. Have you ever had a setback that actually led to a bigger or better opportunity down the line? How did bouncing back shape who you are today?

4. If you were to make your own 'Think Different' campaign, who would be your personal 'crazy ones' – the people who inspire you to be bold and original?
What can you learn from their example?

> **I've always respected those who tried to change the world for the better, rather than just complain about it.**

Michael Bloomberg

CHAPTER 5
UPWARD MOMENTUM
OPTIMISM

A number of years ago, I had one of those unforgettable moments watching NASA's InSight probe land on Mars, live on TV. I mean, how often do you get to witness something so astonishing? Here they were, sending a robot 33.9 million miles away to uncover the secrets of another planet's insides. The mission wasn't just about science – it was about daring to dream big and making it happen.

The goal of the InSight mission was ambitious: to study Mars' core, crust and mantle. Scientists wanted to understand how Mars formed around 4.6 billion years ago when the solar system was just getting started. By digging (literally) into Mars' past, they hoped to uncover clues about how rocky planets like Earth came to be.

The adventure began on 5 May, 2018, when the InSight spacecraft launched from California aboard a rocket. This was no ordinary journey – this was a seven-month journey through space at an extraordinary speed of 6,200 miles per hour.

When it finally arrived at Mars, things got intense. The spacecraft had to pull off what NASA calls the "seven minutes of terror"

– a high-stakes landing sequence that's as nerve-racking as it sounds. InSight entered the Martian atmosphere at 12,300 mph and had to slow down to a gentle 5 mph before touching down safely. How did it manage that? With a combination of parachutes, retro-thrusters, and a heat shield that kept it from burning up during re-entry.

Landing on Mars is far from straightforward – only about 40% of missions actually succeed. But thanks to years of planning and teamwork by thousands of scientists and engineers, InSight made it. And when those first signals came back confirming the landing? Let's just say the celebrations at NASA were unmistakable!

Once safely on the Martian surface, InSight got straight to work. It deployed two key instruments:

1. **A seismometer** – This device listened for "Mars quakes," which are earthquakes, but on Mars. By studying these quakes, scientists could learn more about the planet's interior structure.

2. **A heat probe** – This tool burrowed into the ground to measure how heat flows beneath the surface, offering insights into Mars' geological history.

Achieving something as complex as the InSight mission takes more than just technical know-how – it takes optimism, and loads of it. Why? Because space exploration is full of challenges, setbacks and moments where things don't go according to plan. Without optimism, it would be easy to give up when things get tough.

Anne Kinney, a director from NASA's Goddard Space Flight Centre, summed it up perfectly: "If you have a method or idea and you believe it works, you have to be optimistic about it. Optimism is the number one thing."

Optimism is essential for solving problems that seem impossible at first glance. It's what keeps teams motivated when they're facing daunting odds or working on projects that take years (or even decades) to complete.

HOW LEADERS CAN LEARN OPTIMISM

So, here's the key question: can optimism be learned? According to Dr Martin Seligman – a psychology professor at the University of Pennsylvania – the answer is yes! He developed something called the **ABCDE model** of learned optimism, which is a step-by-step guide for cultivating a more positive mindset. The model works as follows:

1. **Adversity** – Start by identifying the challenge or problem you're facing. For the InSight team, this included stressful moments like designing a spacecraft that could survive entry into Mars' atmosphere or troubleshooting issues during testing.

2. **Belief** – Take an honest look at your thoughts and feelings about this challenge. Are you feeling confident? Doubtful? The InSight team had to believe in their abilities and trust that their hard work would pay off.

3. **Consequence** – Reflect on how your beliefs shape your actions and decisions. For example, believing in their mission helped the team stay focused and resilient during setbacks.

4. **Disputation** – Challenge any negative beliefs by looking for evidence that contradicts them. When doubts crept in (as they inevitably do), NASA's engineers reminded themselves of past successes and relied on their expertise.

5. **Energization** – Notice how this process changes your perspective and motivation levels. For the InSight team, every small victory – like successful tests or milestones – reinforced their optimism and kept them motivated.

By applying this model, leaders can develop a more optimistic outlook that inspires confidence in their teams – even during tough times.

WHY OPTIMISM IS CRITICAL FOR LEADERS

Optimism isn't just about feeling positive; it's transformative for leadership. Here's why optimistic leaders have an edge:

- **It's contagious** – When leaders stay positive, their team picks up on that energy, too. Suddenly, even big challenges feel manageable because everyone believes success is possible.

- **It fuels creativity** – Optimistic leaders encourage creative thinking because they're open to exploring fresh solutions instead of fixating on problems.

- **It builds trust** – Seeing potential in people (rather than focusing on flaws) helps leaders build stronger relationships with their teams.

- **It boosts resilience** – Optimistic leaders bounce back from setbacks faster – and show their teams how to do the same.

But let's be clear: optimism isn't about ignoring reality or pretending everything is fine when it's not. It's about balancing realism with hope – acknowledging challenges while focusing on solutions.

LESSONS FROM INSIGHT: EMBRACING OPTIMISM IN EVERYDAY LIFE

The InSight mission wasn't just a triumph of science; it was proof that optimism can achieve remarkable things. Whether you're leading a team at work or tackling personal goals, there are plenty of lessons we can take from NASA's approach:

1. **Think ambitiously but stay grounded** – Like NASA engineers who dared to imagine exploring another planet while meticulously planning every detail.

2. **Don't fear failure** – Remember that only 40% of Mars missions succeed – but each attempt brings valuable lessons for future efforts.

3. **Appreciate progress** – Every milestone matters! Recognizing progress along the way keeps motivation high.

4. **Stay curious** – Whether you're studying Mars' interior or solving everyday problems here on Earth, curiosity is key.

THE SEVEN MINUTES OF TERROR

Cruise Stage Separation
Time: Entry - 7 mins

Entry Turn Starts
Time: Entry - 6.5 mins (Turn completed by Entry - 5 min)

Entry
Altitude: 80 miles (128 km) Velocity: 13,200 mph (5,900 metres/sec)

Peak Heating
44.2 watts per square centimetre

Peak Deceleration
7.4 g (before chute)

Parachute Deployment
Altitude: 7.5 miles (12 km) Velocity: 928 mph (415 metres/sec) Time: Entry + 223 sec

Heat Shield Jettison
Altitude: 6.4 miles (10.3 km) Velocity: 295 mph (132 metres/sec) Time: Entry + 238 sec

Leg Deployments
Time: Entry + 248 sec

Radar Activated
Altitude: 3.4 miles (5.5 km) Time: Entry + 300 sec

Radar First Acquisition
Altitude: 1.4 miles (2.3 km) Time: Touchdown - 61 sec

Lander Separation
Altitude: 0.7 miles (1.1 km) Velocity: 136 mph (61 metres/sec) Time: Touchdown - 43 sec

Gravity Turn Start
Altitude: 0.6 miles (0.9 km) Time: Touchdown - 40 sec

Constant Velocity Start
Altitude: 167 feet (51 metres) Velocity: 17 mph (7.8 metres/sec) Time: Touchdown - 16 sec

Touchdown

Source: https://www.jpl.nasa.gov/news/press_kits/insight/launch/mission/

The story of NASA's InSight mission is more than just a tale of space exploration – it's a testament to what humans can achieve when we combine optimism with hard work and determination. From overcoming "seven minutes of terror" during landing to uncovering ancient secrets buried beneath Mars' surface, this mission proved that even the biggest challenges are conquerable with enough grit and positivity.

So next time life throws you an unexpected challenge – or maybe even your own version of "seven minutes of terror" – remember this: with optimism giving you the empathetic edge, you've got what it takes to succeed!

THE BIG QUESTIONS

1. What's the most ambitious goal you've ever dreamed up, something that felt as wild as landing a robot on Mars? What would it take to actually start working towards it?

2. The InSight team faced "seven minutes of terror" during the landing. When was the last time you had to stay calm and focused during a highly stressful moment? How did you handle it?

3. Only about 40% of Mars missions actually succeed. What's something big you've tried - even if you knew it might not work out?
What did you learn from trying?

4. The InSight mission was all about teamwork and daring to dream big. Who's on your 'mission control' team, the people who help you go after your biggest goals?
How do you celebrate wins together?

> **Whether you think you can, or you think you can't – you're right.**

Henry Ford

CHAPTER 6
PREDICTING THE FUTURE
MINDSET

Consider one of the most successful and fascinating entrepreneurs of all time – Bill Gates. You know him as the co-founder of Microsoft, one of the figures who helped bring personal computing into the mainstream, and one of the richest people on the planet. The key point is this: Gates isn't just a tech genius. He's also a master of adaptability, learning from mistakes, and leading with a growth mindset. His story is packed with lessons that can make you rethink how you approach leadership.

Let's rewind to 1975. Gates and his childhood friend Paul Allen started Microsoft with just two employees and a dream. Fast-forward to today, and Microsoft has grown into one of the most valuable companies in the world, employing over 228,000 people as of 2024. Millions of us use Microsoft products daily – whether it's Word for work, Teams for meetings, or Xbox for relaxing after a long day.

So how did Gates turn a small startup into a global tech giant? Sure, he's brilliant at coding and business strategy – but his secret weapon is his mindset. Gates doesn't just see challenges; he sees opportunities. And when things don't go as planned, he adapts.

In his 1999 book *Business @ The Speed of Thought*, Gates made some bold predictions about where technology was headed. Some seemed ambitious at the time, but they turned out to be spot-on. For example, he predicted that people would carry small devices to stay connected and conduct business from anywhere. Sound familiar? Today, we've got smartphones, tablets and smartwatches doing exactly that.

He also foresaw tailored online advertising – you know those eerily accurate ads that pop up on Facebook or Instagram? He even predicted how constant connectivity would reshape how we work and live.

Of course, even geniuses get it wrong sometimes. In 1994, Gates famously doubted the commercial potential of the internet. Instead of doubling down on his mistake or pretending he never said it, he pivoted. He recognized the internet's importance and shifted Microsoft's focus accordingly. That ability to adapt is what makes Gates such an exceptional leader.

FIXED VS GROWTH MINDSET: WHAT KIND OF LEADER ARE YOU?

Gates' success isn't just about his intelligence – it's about his particular mindset. Stanford University psychologist Carol Dweck calls this a "growth mindset." In simple terms:

- **Fixed Mindset**: People with this mindset believe their abilities are set in stone. They see failure as proof they're not good enough and avoid risks because they're afraid of looking bad.

- **Growth Mindset**: People with this mindset believe they can improve through effort and learning. They see failure as a stepping stone to success and embrace challenges as opportunities to grow.

"Failure is an opportunity to grow"

GROWTH MINDSET

"I can learn to do anything I want"

"Challenges help me to grow"

"My effort and attitude determine my abilities"

"Feedback is constructive"

"I am inspired by the success of others"

"I like to try new things"

"Failure is the limit of my abilities"

FIXED MINDSET

"I'm either good at it or I'm not"

"My abilities are unchanging"

"I can either do it, or I can't"

"I don't like to be challenged"

"My potential is predetermined"

"When I'm frustrated, I give up"

"Feedback and criticism are personal"

"I stick to what I know"

So how does this play out in leadership? Let's compare:

	FIXED MINDSET	**GROWTH MINDSET**
RESPONSE TO FAILURE	"I messed up; I'm no good at this."	"I messed up; what can I learn from this?"
PROBLEM-SOLVING	Sticks to what they know; avoids innovative approaches.	Welcomes creativity; encourages experimentation.
EFFORT	Sees effort as proof they're inadequate ("If I were good at this, I wouldn't have to try so hard.")	Sees effort as essential for improvement.
RESPONSE TO FEEDBACK	"They're criticizing me because I'm not good enough."	"This feedback will help me improve and get better."
COMPETITION	They're better than me; I'll never catch up."	"I got inopiration in others' achievements, and I use them as motivation to grow."
CHALLENGES TO FAILURE	"I am going to avoid tough tasks because I will probably fail."	"I am excited to tackle challenges head-on, as I see them as opportunities to learn and develop."
LEARNING NEW SKILLS	"I'm just not talented at this; there's no point in trying."	"I might struggle now, but with practice, I'll get better."

These examples highlight how adopting a growth mindset fosters resilience, adaptability, and continuous improvement in various aspects of life.

WHY GROWTH MINDSET MATTERS

The truth is leaders who embrace challenges instead of fearing them, and who see failures as learning opportunities, create environments where their teams feel safe to embrace bold ideas and drive change.

Gates is a perfect example of this in action. When faced with setbacks (like underestimating the internet), he didn't walk away or blame others. Instead, he adapted, learned from his mistakes and turned them into opportunities for growth.

This kind of resilience doesn't just benefit leaders – it inspires teams to push past their own limits, too. Leaders with a growth mindset are well placed for this because they model resilience and adaptability.

When you embrace challenges instead of fearing them, and when you show your team that mistakes are just part of learning, it inspires everyone.

When things don't go to plan, be prepared to pivot, as Gates did, or reframe challenges like Dweck suggests. It will give you the empathetic edge. Remember: leadership isn't about being perfect – it's about helping others shine their brightest while growing alongside them.

And who knows? Maybe one day someone will tell *your story* in their leadership masterclass!

THE BIG QUESTIONS

1. When you hit a roadblock, do you see it as a dead end or as a chance to try something new, like Bill Gates does? How could shifting your mindset help you spot new opportunities?

2. What's something impressive your team has accomplished together that you couldn't have pulled off solo? How did everyone's different mindsets help make it happen?

3. How do you react when things don't go as planned? Can you think of a time when adapting in the moment led to a surprising win?

4. Gates is known for learning from mistakes and bouncing back. What's one lesson you've learned from a past mistake that's actually helped you become better at what you do?

> **Timing, perseverance, and ten years of trying will eventually make you look like an overnight success.**

Biz Stone

CHAPTER 7
FROM FRUSTRATION TO INNOVATION
PERSEVERANCE

James Dyson's story isn't your typical tale of perseverance and determination – it's about vacuum cleaners. And somehow, it's surprisingly inspiring. Dyson's journey proves that with enough determination (and a staggering number of prototypes), you can turn frustration into innovation and failure into success.

It all started in the late 1970s when Dyson got fed up with traditional vacuums losing suction as their bags filled up. Most people would grumble and move on, but not Dyson. Inspired by industrial cyclone technology used in factories to separate dust from air, he thought, "Why not use this to make a bagless vacuum?" It was a simple but powerful idea. But turning it into reality was an extraordinarily complex challenge.

Over five years, Dyson built 5,127 prototypes. Yes, FIVE THOUSAND ONE HUNDRED AND TWENTY-SEVEN. Each one failed in some way, but instead of giving up, Dyson treated every failure as a lesson. Prototype 4 didn't work? No problem – he'd tweak it and try again. Prototype 1567 didn't work? – again, not a problem. Prototype 4256 yep, you guessed it – didn't work? Guess what he tried straight away!

But finally, success, as in 1993, his persistence paid off with the world's first bagless vacuum cleaner: the Dyson Dual Cyclone.

But the road wasn't smooth yet. UK manufacturers rejected his invention largely because they didn't want to lose their lucrative vacuum bag business. Undeterred, Dyson took his design to Japan, where it became a hit. His vacuum won awards and they sold for around £1,600 at the time. With this success under his belt, he launched his own company and turned Dyson into a household name.

Even after his big break, Dyson didn't rest on his laurels. His original DC01 vacuum has been redesigned over 50 times since its debut in 1993 because he believes there's always room for improvement. His company now creates bladeless fans, hand dryers, air purifiers and hair dryers, all with clever engineering and sleek designs.

What makes Dyson truly inspiring is his view on failure. To him, mistakes aren't setbacks, they're stepping stones to success. His story reminds us that persistence pays off and that every failure is just another chance to learn something new. The lesson is simple: persistence matters; channel your inner James Dyson and keep going!

perseverance

[pər-sə-vir-əns] noun • *English*

---

persistence in doing something despite difficulty or delay in achieving success. the ability to finish what you committed to regardless of obstacles that stand on the way.

WHY PERSEVERANCE MATTERS

Empathetic leadership might sound like something often dismissed as 'soft' leadership, but it's actually one of the best ways to lead a team. It's all about being human, showing understanding, compassion, and creating a workplace where people feel like they're more than just cogs in a machine. In practice, even the most empathetic leaders have their work cut out for them when times get tough. Keeping everyone motivated when things aren't going so well? That's where perseverance plays a crucial role.

Determination is basically the ability to keep going when you hit a wall (or ten). For empathetic leaders, it's the crucial thing that helps them stick to their vision while lifting their team up during rough patches. Even better, when leaders show they're not giving up, their teams tend to follow suit. Suddenly, you've got a culture of resilience and determination that can handle pretty much anything life throws at it.

Let's break this down into bite-sized chunks because perseverance is like a highly versatile leadership skill – it does so much.

1. IT MAKES TEAMS TOUGHER

Your team hits a big snag in a project. Everyone's stressed, but then your leader steps up and says, "We'll work through this. Let's figure it out." That attitude quickly spreads! When leaders show they can handle challenges without crumbling, their teams start thinking the same way. Setbacks stop feeling like failures and start looking like puzzles to solve.

2. IT CREATES A "WE CAN DO ANYTHING" CULTURE

Standing firm isn't just about powering through – it's about shifting how people see obstacles. Instead of panicking over setbacks, teams learn to see them as chances to grow and improve. This kind of mindset sparks creativity and teamwork because everyone feels safe enough to throw ideas into the mix.

3. IT BUILDS TRUST

Here's the thing: when leaders stick by their teams during tough times, it sends a clear message – "You're not on your own." That builds trust quickly. Employees feel valued and supported, which makes them more engaged and ready to give their best.

THE IMPACT OF PERSEVERANCE

When empathetic leaders embrace perseverance, clear benefits begin to emerge – not just for them but for their teams too:

- **Better Performance**: Teams that keep pushing forward tend to hit their goals even when things get tough.

- **Happier Employees**: A supportive work environment makes people feel appreciated and happy employees stick around longer.

- **More Creativity**: Perseverance encourages people to think outside the box and come up with fresh ideas instead of giving up.

Let's face it: today's world moves fast and unexpected challenges pop up left and right. Empathetic leaders who know how to endure are better equipped to handle those setbacks while keeping their teams motivated and focused. They inspire resilience, spark innovation and build trust, all the while driving success.

But don't think determination is just about grinding through tough times; it's also about staying flexible enough to adapt while focused on the end goal. It's like being a GPS that recalculates when there's traffic but still gets everyone to their destination.

Yes, empathetic leadership is about connection and understanding, but without perseverance, even the best intentions can fall flat when challenges arise. By sticking with their vision and supporting their teams through adversity, empathetic leaders create strong foundations for success that give them that edge.

Think of determination as the glue that holds everything together – it keeps empathetic leadership grounded while pushing teams forward towards growth and achievement. And when you mix perseverance with resilience you get a powerful combination that drives positive change.

So, whether you're leading a team or just trying to navigate your own challenges at work (or life), remember this: setbacks aren't roadblocks – they're stepping stones. With empathy, determination and perseverance on your side, there's no limit to what you can achieve.

THE BIG QUESTIONS

1. Can you think of a time when you kept trying at something, even after several failures, and finally had a breakthrough?
   What kept you going?

2. Dyson built over 5,000 prototypes before hitting success. What's something in your life or work that you'd stick with, even if it took many attempts to get it right?

3. How do you usually react when things don't go as planned? Do you get frustrated, or do you see it as a chance to learn and try again?
   How could you bring more of that 'learn and try again' attitude to your team?

4. Perseverance and empathy go hand in hand for great leaders. How can you show your team that you'll support them, especially when things get tough?

> **Success comes from knowing what you do best and doing it.**

Mark Cuban

CHAPTER 8
LEADING THROUGH STRENGTHS
STRENGTHS

Let me introduce you to Sarah and her journey at Starbucks.

When Sarah first joined as a barista, she saw it simply as a way to pay the bills. What she didn't realize was that the green apron would mark the beginning of a career she had never imagined.

From day one, Sarah discovered that Starbucks was about far more than making coffee. It was about connection, development and opportunity. She wasn't simply handed an apron and left to figure things out – she received structured training, from mastering coffee craft to delivering great customer experiences.

Along the way, Sarah realized she had a natural ability to solve problems and connect with people. Her managers noticed too, offering encouragement and a gentle nudge: "You've got real potential."

Through workshops, leadership development and initiatives such as the Starbucks College Achievement Plan, opportunities continued to open up. Her commitment and growth didn't go unnoticed. She was recognized as Partner of the Quarter, Starbucks' term for employees, which gave her the confidence to aim higher.

Before long, Sarah was doing far more than making coffee. She was supporting colleagues, mentoring new starters and helping to run store operations with confidence and professionalism.

Eventually, her leadership capabilities caught the attention of senior leaders. Through Starbucks' succession planning programs, she stepped into a management role, overseeing multiple stores. What set her apart was her ability to treat customers and colleagues with genuine care, while remaining focused, innovative and driven.

Sarah reflects on her journey with pride. Starbucks didn't just give her a job, it gave her the opportunity to grow. Through mentorship, development programs and consistent support, her story shows what's possible when organizations invest in their people.

So next time you sip your latte, remember: behind every cup is someone like Sarah, a partner whose strengths are recognized, nurtured and celebrated.

And strengths is the focus for this chapter!

As we have explored already, empathetic leadership might sound like something out of a motivational seminar, but really, it's just about being a decent human being. It's all about understanding, compassion and openness by creating a workplace where people feel seen, heard and valued. And when leaders identify their own unique strengths, and those of their team, they can take things to the next level. Think stronger relationships, better teamwork and an atmosphere where everyone actually *wants* to work together. This creates stronger, more effective teams.

LET'S TALK STRENGTHS

Okay, let's start with the basics – what do we mean by strengths? Some call them strengths, others call them gifts or talents, but whatever you call them, they're the core capabilities that make empathetic leaders perform at their best. Strengths are those natural abilities that help people connect, inspire and lead in ways that make their teams feel like high performers.

Just reflect for a minute on something you have ever done and thought, "Wow, this just feels right!" That's your strengths at work. A strength is basically one of those personal traits that makes you feel energized, confident and working at your strongest. It's like your key advantage for doing your best work at whatever you do. When you lean into your strengths, things just click – you perform better, feel happier, and honestly, life just gets a little easier.

So, let's use Sarah's Starbucks' journey to show how she used three of her natural strengths to grow, develop and progress.

COMMUNICATION

Think of a leader who explains things so clearly you actually 'get' it. That's the magic of communication. Empathetic leaders with this talent don't just talk – they listen. Whether Sarah was mentoring teammates or chatting with customers, she knew how to share ideas and address concerns while making everyone feel heard.

ADAPTABILITY

Every team is like a mixed bag of personalities, quirks and working styles. Leaders with adaptability know how to respond effectively – they're those who remain calm and adjust their approach to fit the team's needs. Sarah showed off this talent when she took on new responsibilities and learned how to manage store operations while mentoring others. Whether it's revisiting deadlines or adjusting communication styles, adaptability is about making things work with calm and confidence.

STRATEGIC THINKING

Strategic thinking helps leaders juggle big-picture goals while keeping their team's emotional wellbeing in check. Think of Sarah stepping into her managerial role; she wasn't just running stores – she was driving team success while treating everyone like family.

Sarah's story shows how recognizing your strengths can take you from brewing coffee to leading teams, and it all starts with understanding what makes you effective.

So next time you order your Starbucks cappuccino, take a moment to think about the person behind the counter; someone using their strengths to make your day (and your coffee) just a little better!

HOW STRENGTHS SUPERCHARGE LEADERSHIP

Here's the important point: your strengths are yours, and your team's strengths are theirs. Each person brings something different. When leaders understand those differences and put strengths to work deliberately, performance improves and teams function at their best.

Empathetic leaders know how to make their teams grow, develop and progress, just as Sarah did, and as a result, the extraordinary unfolds. These are the clear benefits:

- **Team engagement increases significantly:** When leaders understand what their team needs, people feel motivated and invested in their work. Suddenly, it's not just about hitting deadlines – it's about being part of something bigger.

- **Collaboration becomes second nature**: Strengths like communication and adaptability create an environment where teamwork thrives. People feel comfortable sharing ideas because they know their contributions matter.

- **Conflicts are more manageable**: Let's be realistic, every workplace has its share of challenges. But empathetic leaders know how to smooth things over and maintain harmony.

- **Retention rates increase**: Employees stick around when they feel valued and supported. Empathy fosters loyalty and, let's face it, who doesn't want to work for someone who genuinely cares and promotes using their strengths every day?

HOW TO DISCOVER YOUR STRENGTHS AND THOSE OF YOUR TEAM

You may be wondering, "Sure, strengths sound great, and I get the Sarah example, but how do I actually figure mine out, and more importantly, my team's?" This is where these tools can help people identify their strengths. Two of the most popular ones are:

- **Gallup Strengths Finder** – Gallup interviewed 1.7 million people (yes, million) across all kinds of jobs – teachers, lawyers, nurses, students—you name it. From that research, they identified 34 key 'strength themes' and built an assessment tool to help you figure out what suits you best. To date, over 30 million people have used it.

- **VIA (Values in Action) Character Strengths** – Another effective tool for understanding what fuels your strengths and performance. These 24 character strengths fall under six broad categories of wisdom, courage, humanity, justice, temperance and transcendence.

If you're more of a book person, check out *The Strengths Book* by Sally Bibb or *StrengthsFinder 2.0* by Tom Rath and Gallup. These books not only break down the science behind strengths but also give practical tips on how to use them in real life.

Tools and books are amazing, but having someone to talk it through with is crucial. A coach or mentor who is experienced and can help you dig deeper into what your strengths really mean and how to use them to make an impact in your life (and work) and on your teams. You can search for accredited Gallup Strength Finders or VIA coaches or mentors who know what they're doing.

And don't forget your support network – your family and friends. Ask them what they think you're naturally good at. Not things like, "You're good at Excel," but qualities such as:

"You're incredibly adaptable – you manage competing demands with ease."

"You're a strong communicator – you have a real ability to make people feel heard."

"You have a natural talent for bringing people together."

"You consistently come up with creative ideas – it's genuinely inspiring!"

Sometimes the people around us see our strengths more clearly than we do ourselves.

And take a moment for self-reflection so that you don't forget about 'the real you.' Deep down, you probably already know what truly energizes you. Think about the parts of your job or your hobbies that make you excited – the things that make time fly by because you're so in the zone. What do people compliment you on? What tasks feel effortless but still get amazing results? Those are clear indicators of your strengths.

The point is this: when you focus on what you're naturally good at – your strengths – you unlock your full potential, and consequently as a leader you unlock the full potential of your team. It's not about fixing weaknesses or being good at everything; it's about focusing more deliberately on what makes you 'you.' So go ahead – take that assessment, read that book, or have that conversation with your mentor or coach. Discovering your strengths isn't just fun – it's empowering.

By leveraging your strengths, and those of your teams, you will build stronger dynamic teams that perform better together, leading you to achieve that empathetic edge in everything you do.

THE BIG QUESTIONS

1. What's one strength you use at work that just feels right and energizes you, like Sarah with her communication or adaptability?

2. How have you helped someone on your team grow, feel valued or step up lately, maybe by mentoring or just being in their corner?

3. When things change or get hectic, how do you stay flexible and help create a positive environment for your team?

4. If your co-workers described your 'unique formula' as a leader, what would they say makes you stand out, and how do you want to use that even more?

> **Failure is not the opposite of success; it's part of success.**

Arianna Huffington

CHAPTER 9
LEARNING THROUGH FAILURE
FAILURE

Meet Reshma Saujani, founder of Girls Who Code and a powerful example of how failure can quietly reshape a life. Her story shows that losing isn't always an ending as sometimes it's a turning point.

In 2010, Reshma was working as a successful lawyer, with degrees from Harvard and Yale. On paper, her life looked complete. Yet beneath that success, she felt unsettled. She wanted her work to matter more, to reach further. So she made a difficult choice and ran for Congress in New York.

It wasn't easy. She campaigned relentlessly, knocking on doors, speaking to voters, and putting herself forward in a space where she didn't naturally belong. When the election came, she lost. Not narrowly, but decisively.

For many people, that kind of loss would have been discouraging enough to stop altogether. But Reshma saw it differently. Later, she reflected that the worst part of losing an election is simply losing, and the best part is the freedom it gives you to pursue what truly matters.

That realization pushed her toward an issue she deeply cared about: the lack of women in technology. In 2012, she founded Girls Who Code, a non-profit dedicated to teaching girls technical skills and helping them develop confidence, curiosity and resilience.

More than a decade later, the organization has reached over 90,000 girls across the United States, helping to open doors in an industry long dominated by men. It has also helped shape a generation that sees failure not as something to fear, but as something to learn from.

Reshma's story reminds us that failure doesn't define us – it redirects us. Sometimes, what feels like a setback is simply the space we need to begin again, more honestly and with greater purpose.

SUCCESS

HARD WORK
PERSISTENCE
LATE NIGHTS
REJECTIONS
SACRIFICES
DISCIPLINE
CRITICISM
DOUBTS
FAILURE
RISKS

WHY FAILURE IS SO IMPORTANT

In truth, failure gets a bad reputation. It's the thing we dread, the word we avoid, and the experience we'd rather not talk about. But here's the point: failure isn't the enemy in your story – it's actually one of the key things you weren't aware you need to achieve the empathetic edge. Failure isn't simply a bump in the road; it's a springboard for creativity, resilience and growth.

So, let's explore why failure deserves a second look. It's not as difficult as it seems, and it might just be the best thing that ever happens to you.

First things first: let's stop treating failure as the end of the world. Yes, it can hurt. It can knock your confidence and leave you wanting to retreat for a while. But the truth is, failure often marks the beginning of something meaningful – a chance to learn, adjust and move forward with greater clarity.

Take Thomas Edison, for example, the person who invented the light bulb. Edison famously said, "I have not failed 10,000 times, I've successfully found 10,000 ways that will not work." Is that not a better way to look at it? Edison didn't see his mistakes as defeats; he saw them as experiments. And guess what? Those experiments eventually paid off.

Empathetic leaders know this better than anyone. They understand that every mistake is nothing but another step towards success, and they embrace failure as part of the process.

FAILURE SPARKS CREATIVITY

Here's an interesting fact: failure often acts as a catalyst for creativity. When things don't go according to plan, you're forced to think outside the box and come up with new solutions. Empathetic leaders thrive in these moments because they see failure as an invitation to innovate rather than a reason to give up.

Look at Sara Blakely, founder of Spanx. Before she became a self-made entrepreneur, she faced rejection after rejection from manufacturers who didn't believe in her product. Instead of giving up, Sara got creative – she pitched her idea directly to department stores and even demonstrated her prototype herself. Her willingness to embrace failure led her to revolutionize an industry and build a successful business.

So next time you hit a wall, take a page from Sara's story: think creatively, stay curious, and remember that failure can often lead to new ideas.

FAILURE BUILDS RESILIENCE

Let's look at resilience – the ability to bounce back after setbacks. It's one of life's most underrated attributes, and guess what? Failure is how you build it. Every time you fall flat on your face and pick yourself back up, you're strengthening your mental toughness; like any skill, it strengthens with practice.

Empathetic leaders don't see failure as a reflection of their worth; they see it as feedback on their process. They know that resilience keeps them grounded and it reminds them that success doesn't happen overnight but requires hard work and persistence.

Think about Oprah Winfrey – she was fired from her first TV job for being 'too emotional.' Instead of letting this setback define her career, she leaned into her ability to connect deeply with people, a skill that ultimately made her one of the most beloved media personalities in history.

Failure hurts, no doubt about it – but every time you rise again, you're proving to yourself (and everyone else) that you can handle it.

FAILURE FOSTERS EMPATHY

Here's an unexpected benefit: failing makes you more empathetic. Experiencing setbacks helps leaders understand what their teams are going through when things don't go as planned. It builds compassion and allows them to offer genuine encouragement.

Empathetic leaders don't just brush off failure; they share their own stories of struggle to inspire their teams. Failure isn't just about learning lessons; it's about connecting with others who are going through tough times and reminding them that they're not alone.

FAILURE CREATES OPPORTUNITIES

Believe it or not, failure can open doors you never expected. Every time you fail, you're forced to reassess your approach, and sometimes that leads you down an entirely new path filled with possibilities.

Take J.K. Rowling, for example. Before publishing *Harry Potter*, she faced massive rejection from publishers who didn't believe in her story. But those failures helped her refine her craft and ultimately build one of the most beloved literary franchises in history.

Empathetic leaders understand this well. They don't shy away from setbacks, knowing that difficult moments often make later successes more meaningful.

THE VALUE OF FAILURE

Let's be honest: success feels way better when you've earned it through struggle. If everything came easily all the time, would we even appreciate our wins? Failure teaches us to value success because we've seen how hard it is to achieve.

Consider Richard Branson and the remarkable empire he has built under the Virgin brand – Virgin Atlantic, Virgin Galactic, Virgin Records and Virgin Money, to name a few. However, his journey hasn't been without setbacks. Ventures like Virgin Student, Virgin Cars, Virgin Brides and Virgin Cola all failed to take off.

Reflecting on these experiences, the Virgin Group founder once said in an interview: "Whether it is launching companies like Virgin Brides and Virgin Cola that fell flat on their face, making the wrong call on investments, or simply forgetting to return a call or send an email, I have made hundreds of mistakes. I'm sure I'll make many more this year and learn valuable lessons from every error."

There's nothing better than succeeding after periods of failure – it's like finally reaching the top of a mountain after climbing through storms and up sheer rockfaces.

FAILURE + POSITIVE THINKING = GROWTH

Here's where positivity comes into play: empathetic leaders don't just accept failure – they embrace it with optimism. They see every setback as an opportunity for growth rather than a reason for despair.

Positive thinking doesn't mean ignoring reality or pretending everything is fine when it isn't – it means choosing to focus on solutions instead of problems. It means believing that every mistake brings you closer to success instead of further away from it.

Jacinda Ardern exemplified this during her tenure as Prime Minister of New Zealand. Even during crises like COVID-19 or natural disasters, she approached challenges with empathy and optimism, showing how positivity can help leaders navigate tough times while inspiring others.

FINAL THOUGHTS: LEARNING FROM FAILURE

Failure isn't as frightening as we think. It often shows up unannounced, but it rarely leaves without teaching us something meaningful. It builds resilience, sparks creativity, fosters empathy, opens unexpected doors, makes success taste much better and encourages positive thinking. For empathetic leaders, failure isn't just a detour; it's an essential part of the journey.

Instead of running from failure, why not embrace it? When life throws you a setback, remember that every misstep can bring you closer to growth. Failure isn't the end of the road; it's the beginning of something better. It's where you find that empathetic edge helping you to learn, grow, and discover your true potential and that of your teams.

So go ahead and take the risk, learn quickly and keep going because the lessons you will get from failure will be priceless.

THE BIG QUESTIONS

1. When was the last time you took a big risk, even if it didn't work out? What did you learn from that experience, and how did it shape what you did next?

2. How do you usually react when things don't go as planned? Do you bounce back like Reshma, or do you need some time to reset first?

3. Can you think of a 'failure' that actually opened up a new opportunity or helped you discover something you're passionate about?

4. How could you use your own stories of setbacks to inspire or support others on your team when they're facing tough times?

> **You don't get lucky. You make your own luck ... Luck happens when you work hard.**

Sara Blakely

CHAPTER 10
THE SERENDIPITOUS ROOM ASSIGNMENT
LUCK

Let's go back to 1983. Picture the scene: Hickory, California, with no hint of what lay ahead. There, a paper salesperson and a maths teacher welcome baby Chris into the world. Meanwhile, in White Plains, New York, a dentist and a psychiatrist are celebrating the arrival of baby Mark. Just a week later, in Gainesville, Florida, another psychiatrist-teacher couple were busy settling in with their newborn son, Dustin.

At this point, none of these families have the faintest idea that their babies will someday cross paths in a way that will change how the world connects. The parents are probably more focused on nappies and midnight feedings than on the future of social media. But as luck would have it, the future had something unexpected ahead for Chris, Mark and Dustin.

Eighteen years later, Chris, Mark and Dustin survive high school and go on to Harvard. It's the end of their freshman year, and they're preparing for year two. If you've ever been to university, you know this is when things start to get underway: you've found your favourite bars and pubs, figured out which lectures to avoid, and maybe even started to find your friends.

But first, there's the all-important question: Where will you live next year? Who will you live with? At Harvard, this is decided by what is, in essence, a housing lottery. An accommodation officer runs a computer program that produces a list of names and room numbers – essentially a random allocation process.

On this fateful day, the computer randomly assigns Chris, Mark and Dustin to share a room in H33 at Kirkland House. They check the lists and see they are going to be living together.

At the time, it felt like just another year, just another room on campus. But this random act of room assignment would spark a chain reaction that would ripple across the globe. Because in that Harvard room, through late-night conversations and chance, the seeds of Facebook were planted – all thanks to a little bit of luck and a lot of sheer coincidence.

LUCK AND LEADERSHIP: WHY EMPATHY MATTERS

So, what does this have to do with achieveing the empathetic edge as a leader? Everything.

In reality, when people talk about great leaders, they love to list a range of must-have skills. You know the ones – emotional intelligence, top-notch communication, critical thinking, adaptability and resilience, to name a few. These are some of the tools leaders need to survive and maybe even thrive in an increasingly complex world.

What's often overlooked is this: sometimes, the real difference between a good leader and a genuinely great one comes down to something far less predictable. That factor is luck.

Luck is an unpredictable factor. It's random, unpredictable and totally out of your control. One day you're minding your own business, the next you bump into someone in an elevator who ends up being your biggest client, mentor or even your future co-founder.

Most of us like to think we are the masters of our own destiny, but let's face it – luck plays a larger role than we care to admit. Sometimes it helps us forward; sometimes it trips us up. The trick is learning how to spot it and what to do when it shows up.

The Roman philosopher Seneca had a thoughtful view on luck: "Luck is where opportunity meets preparation." In other words, you cannot control when luck will show up, but you can be ready for it. Think of it like fishing. You cannot make the fish bite, but you can make sure your line is in the water, your bait is fresh and you're paying attention. When the big one bites, you're ready to reel it in.

For leaders, this means you can't manufacture luck out of thin air. But you can prepare yourself and your team so that when luck does come knocking, you're not caught unprepared.

THE "LUCK SKILL SET": PREPARING FOR OPPORTUNITY

So, how do you actually get better at being lucky? It sounds like a contradiction, but it's not. The trick is to cultivate what some call the "luck skill set" – a trio of abilities that help you make the most of every lucky break that comes your way.

1. SPOT THE UNEXPECTED

   Firstly, you've got to keep your eyes peeled for unexpected opportunities. Luck rarely makes a loud entrance. It's more like a whisper in a noisy room – a random conversation, a weird coincidence, or a sudden shift in the market. Leaders who are curious, open-minded and just a little bit inquisitive are the ones who spot these golden moments.

2. JUDGE THE OPPORTUNITY

   Not every opportunity is worth pursuing. The second piece of the puzzle is discernment. Is this opportunity right for you, your team and your mission? Or is it just a distraction dressed up as a golden ticket? Great leaders know how to weigh the pros and cons, trust their gut and make smart decisions, and fast.

3. TAKE THE LEAP

   This is where courage comes in. Luck almost always wants you to step outside your comfort zone. Maybe it means taking a risk, trying something new, or betting on someone who doesn't tick all the usual boxes. This is where self-confidence comes in. You've got to trust your instincts and be willing to jump, even if you're not 100% sure where you'll land.

WHERE LUCK SHOWS UP

- CHANCE
- HARD WORK
- TALENT

CREATING A LUCK-FRIENDLY ENVIRONMENT

Now, you might be thinking, "Okay, but how do I actually make this happen?" The good news is this: you don't need a four-leaf clover or a rabbit's foot. What you do need is a mindset and a workplace culture that welcomes luck with open arms. Here are some ideas to create that luck-friendly environment.

STAY CURIOUS
Curiosity is your best friend. Ask questions, explore new ideas, and don't be afraid to explore beyond familiar territory. The more you learn, the more likely you are to stumble into something amazing.

WIDEN YOUR NETWORK
Luck loves variety. The more people you know from different backgrounds, industries and walks of life, the more likely you are to hear about new opportunities. So go ahead and strike up that random conversation at the bar or connect with someone outside your usual circle.

REFLECT AND LEARN
Every time luck pays you a visit (good or bad), take a moment to reflect. What worked? What didn't? What can you do differently next time? The more you learn from your experiences, the luckier you'll get.

BUILD SELF-CONFIDENCE
And finally, work on your self-confidence. Trust yourself. Trust your team. When opportunity knocks, don't be afraid to answer, even if you're not sure what's on the other side.

THE BOTTOM LINE

The point is this: the luckiest leaders aren't just good at spotting and seizing opportunities – they're also deeply empathetic. They remember that not everyone gets the same lucky breaks. They use their good fortune to lift others up, share opportunities and create a culture where everyone has a shot at success.

Empathetic leaders are humble enough to admit that luck played a role in their journey. They don't hoard opportunities – they spread them around. That's how you build a team that's not just skilled, but also lucky together.

So, the next time you hear someone talk about leadership, remember: it's not just about skills, determination or intelligence. Sometimes, it's about being in the right place at the right time, and being ready to act when luck shows up. Cultivate your luck skill set, lead with empathy, and you'll be amazed at how opportunity presents itself more often.

And, if all else fails, keep your eyes open. You never know when luck might appear unexpectedly on your leadership journey and change everything

THE BIG QUESTIONS

1. How can I remain open to unexpected opportunities and connections that may shape my leadership journey?

2. In what ways am I preparing myself and my team for future changes, even those we cannot foresee?

3. What systems or processes in my organization could be improved to encourage collaboration and innovation?

4. What slight changes can I make to our routines or systems to increase the chances of creative collisions and fresh ideas emerging?

> **The world is starving for new ideas and great leaders who will champion those ideas.**

Lisa Su

CHAPTER 11
THE POWER OF CURIOSITY
CREATIVITY

What happens when organizations give employees the freedom to follow their curiosity and get creative by simply playing around with ideas? Consider Google's legendary '20% time' policy – a deliberate balance of creativity and trust.

Here's how it works: Google decided to let employees spend 20% of their workweek (essentially one day out of five) working on 'whatever' they wanted. Seriously, anything. No micromanaging, no strict rules – just pure, unfiltered exploration. The thinking was simple: if you let smart people chase their passions, amazing things might happen.

Take Gmail, for example. That email service we all rely on? It was born out of this policy. One engineer recognized that email could be really improved and, from that, Gmail was created. Same with Google Maps. Someone got curious about making navigation easier, and now we can't imagine life without it (dramatically reducing the risk of getting lost!).

The atmosphere at Google during these projects wasn't stiff or formal – it was playful. Employees were encouraged to experiment, fail spectacularly and try again. It wasn't about perfection; it was about discovery. And that's the point: by giving people space to explore their curiosity, Google unlocked ideas that had a significant global impact.

Google isn't the only one doing this! Over at 3M, the creators of Post-it Notes, they have a similar '15% time' policy. One day, an employee tinkering with adhesives that weren't sticky enough accidentally invented Post-it Notes. Imagine that – one of the most iconic office supplies ever came from someone experimenting!

These examples prove that when leaders trust their teams to get creative, without pressure or rigid expectations, the results can be extraordinary. Plus, it's more engaging! Who wouldn't want to work somewhere that says, "Go ahead – explore unconventional ideas"? Sometimes curiosity with creativity leads to genius.

THE CREATIVITY GAP: LEADERS KNOW IT BUT CAN'T FIX IT

Leaders, from all walks of life, and even CEOs of small and large enterprises, know creativity is crucial. Surveys from IBM and PwC reveal that most CEOs rank creativity as the number one leadership trait they're looking for. The challenge is this: they struggle to find employees with those innovative skills. PwC even found that 77% of CEOs admitted they have a hard time finding creative talent. So, while leaders understand what innovation is, they often lack the tools to cultivate it within their organizations.

So how do we fix this? How do we keep curiosity-driven creativity alive even when things calm down? Enter empathetic leadership – a decisive factor. Empathetic leaders understand that creativity rarely responds well to rigid rules; it tends to thrive in environments where people feel trusted and supported. They understand that fostering innovation isn't about forcing ideas – it's about giving people the space, tools and encouragement they need to shine.

Here are some ways empathetic leaders can make magic happen.

THE RIGHT LOCATION MATTERS

Creativity thinking doesn't always happen at your desk – it might hit you in a park, a relaxed café, or even while browsing books at your favourite shop. Empathetic leaders encourage employees to find spaces that inspire them. Remote work is perfect for this – let your team work from wherever sparks their imagination! Switching up surroundings has been proven to boost divergent thinking.

SURROUND YOURSELF WITH THE RIGHT PEOPLE
Innovation thrives on diversity where different perspectives lead to fresh ideas. Empathetic leaders create opportunities for employees to interact with people from various backgrounds and disciplines. Whether it's cross-functional collaboration or networking outside the company, these connections can lead to breakthrough moments.

ENCOURAGE EXPERIMENTATION AND RISK-TAKING
As we explored in chapter 9, failure isn't the enemy – it's part of the process! Empathetic leaders foster a culture where trying new things (even if they fail) is celebrated as a learning opportunity. Give your team resources for experimentation, like time for research or access to prototyping tools.

PROMOTE AUTONOMY AND EMPOWERMENT
Micromanaging quickly undermines creativity. Instead, empathetic leaders trust their teams to manage their own workloads and make decisions independently. When people feel ownership over their work, they're more motivated and way more creative.

CREATE PSYCHOLOGICAL SAFETY
Nobody wants to pitch an idea if they're afraid of being judged or shot down. Empathetic leaders build workplaces where employees feel safe sharing their wildest thoughts, even if they seem unconventional or unpopular at first.

OPEN-PLAN OFFICES AND BRAINSTORMING

Open-plan offices are often designed to encourage collaboration, but studies show they often do the opposite when it comes to creativity. Roger Mavity and Stephen Bayley, authors of *How to Steal Fire*, argue that these layouts disrupt solitude (a key ingredient for deep thought) and promote conformity instead of originality.

Group brainstorming sessions can be a double-edged sword if not handled carefully. While they're meant to spark innovation, they can sometimes do the opposite – creating pressure for people to conform or impress rather than share their truly creative ideas. The fear of judgment or the desire to 'fit in' often stifles originality, leaving the best ideas unspoken. And let's not forget the ultimate creativity killers: endless meetings and bureaucratic distractions. Nothing crushes your creative mojo faster than a marathon session of PowerPoint slides or a meeting that could have been in an email. When brainstorming feels more like a chore than an exciting ideafest, it's time to rethink your approach and create an environment where creativity can truly thrive!

So, I am not suggesting that you move out of your current open-plan offices and find premises where everyone gets their own office. No, all you need are the following little strategies which will have a brilliant impact on creativity and innovation and make everyone more curious, and that will be priceless.

CREATE QUIET ZONES

In reality, sometimes you just need peace and quiet to get those genius ideas flowing. Set up soundproof spaces where employees can escape the buzz of the office and dive into deep thought. Think comfy chairs, soft lighting and maybe even a "Do Not Disturb" sign. It's a space designed for focused work.

FLEXIBLE WORKSPACES

Why stick everyone in the same setup? Offer flexibility. Movable desks, modular furniture or even standing workstations. Let employees pick the atmosphere that suits their mood, whether they're collaborating on a big idea or just need some solo time.

OFFER TIME FOR INNOVATION

Take a page from Google's playbook and give employees dedicated time to work on their own ideas. Whether it's one afternoon a week or an hour a day, this freedom lets them chase their curiosity, and who knows? Their side project might just become your company's next big thing.

RECOGNIZE CREATIVE CONTRIBUTIONS

Every creative idea deserves its moment in the spotlight – even the small ones! Whether it's a shoutout in the team meeting or surprise cupcakes for someone who nailed a brainstorming session, celebrating wins keeps morale high and creativity flowing.

BUILD PSYCHOLOGICAL SAFETY

Make your office a judgment-free zone where people feel safe sharing their weirdest, wildest ideas without fear of getting shut down. When employees know they won't be laughed at or criticized, they're way more likely to let their creativity shine.

ADD MOVEMENT TO MEETINGS

Who says meetings have to happen in stuffy conference rooms? Take them outside for walking meetings, or stroll around the office while brainstorming. Movement gets the blood pumping and sometimes, great ideas come when you're literally on your feet.

These changes are practical and effective. By mixing creativity with playfulness and flexibility, empathetic leaders can turn open-plan chaos into an environment where innovation thrives, and improve day-to-day working life.

By creating environments that value exploration, diversity and psychological safety, leaders can unlock their team's full creative potential – not just during crises, but every single day.

And here's the best part: empathetic leadership isn't reserved for 'naturals.' With self-awareness, training and practice, anyone can develop these skills and transform their workplace into one where collaboration, curiosity and creativity flourish and employees genuinely enjoy showing up every day.

Achieving your empathetic edge – a foundation for sustained innovation where creativity thrives as a continuous advantage. And who knows? With empathetic leadership guiding the way, your team might just come up with ideas that make a meaningful difference, or at least make Mondays a little more exciting!

THE BIG QUESTIONS

1. When was the last time you gave yourself (or your team) permission to just experiment with an idea, without worrying about the outcome? What happened?

2. How do you create space for different personalities and work styles on your team, like offering quiet zones, flexible workspaces or time for passion projects?

3. Think about a time when someone (maybe you!) took a risk or tried something new at work. What did you learn from that experience, even if it didn't go as planned?

4. How do you make it secure for people to share their less conventional ideas without fear of judgment? Do you encourage playfulness, or create a supportive environment?

> **Forget about making mistakes, just do it. Surround yourself with friends who will support you and challenge you.**

Richard Branson

CHAPTER 12
THE UNSUNG HEROES
FRIENDSHIP

We've just looked at how creativity influences empathetic leadership. Before we go any further, there's another important element to consider. It's not a skill you can learn from a seminar or a trait you're born with. It's something simpler yet profoundly impactful: 'friends.'

Yes, friends – the people who cheer you on when you're down, and remind you to stop working and go for beer at the pub once in a while. But beyond the fun and camaraderie, friendships are an essential pillar of empathetic leadership. They shape how leaders connect with their teams, navigate challenges and stay grounded in their mission. So let's look at why friends matter more than we often realize, particularly when it comes to leading with empathy.

Because friends are a source of emotional renewal. They help you stay sane when work feels overwhelming and remind you that you're human too.

Remember room H33 in chapter 10 where Facebook was born. Things moved quickly after that. When Facebook was growing faster than he could keep up with, Mark Zuckerberg faced a major existential crisis. Should he sell the company? Should he pivot? He questioned whether to continue at all. At that point, Steve Jobs offered guidance: "Go visit a temple in India."

Zuckerberg took the advice seriously, and that trip helped him reconnect with his vision for Facebook – to connect people around the world. This renewed sense of mission shaped his leadership style and helped Facebook thrive during its most challenging years.

The key point? Friends don't just offer emotional support; they give perspective, clarity, and sometimes even life-changing advice.

THE EIGHT ROLES OF FRIENDS

In Tom Rath's book *Vital Friends*, he identified eight unique roles that your friends can adopt to help you as a leader – kind of like a well-rounded circle of support. Each friend brings their own skills to the table, making them invaluable in different situations. Here are the different types of friends who shape our lives:

- **Builder**: The friend who motivates you to hit your goals. Builders are like that coach who yells, "You've got this!" even when you're gasping for air halfway through a marathon.

- **Champion**: The loyal defender who stands by your side no matter what. Champions speak positively about you in front of others and reinforce confidence and self-belief.

- **Companion**: The friend who's there through good times and bad. Companions provide a sense of comfort – steady, familiar and reliable.

- **Connector**: The networker who introduces you to people and opportunities. Connectors know everyone and can help expand your circle.

- **Collaborator**: The friend who shares your interests and makes teamwork enjoyable. Whether it's a love for books or a passion for politics, collaborators help things fall into place.

- **Energizer**: The friend you turn to for fun who lifts your mood instantly. Energizers bring a sense of positivity and momentum wherever they go.

- **Mind Opener**: The visionary who challenges your thinking and broadens your horizons. Mind openers push you out of your comfort zone in the best way possible.

- **Navigator**: The wise advisor who helps you make tough decisions. Navigators are like GPS for life – they guide you when you're lost.

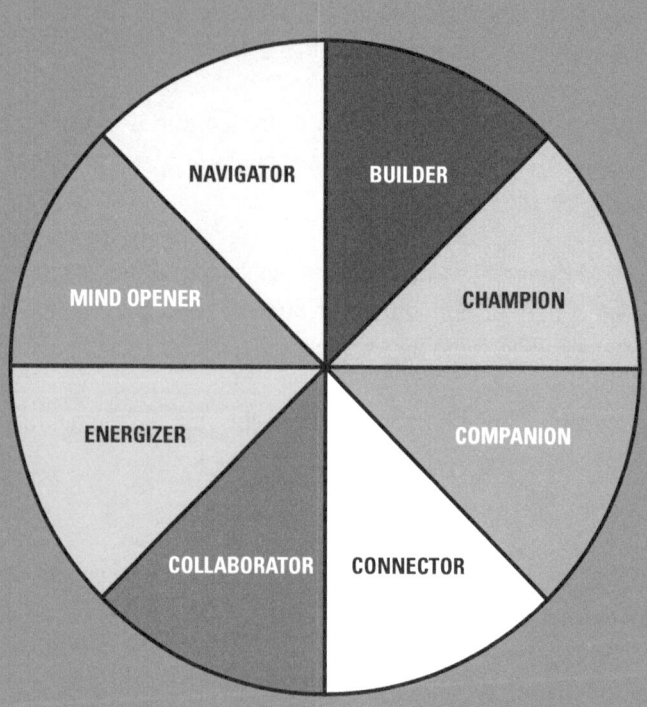

PUTTING FRIENDSHIP INTO ACTION

So how do you actually use these friendship roles as tools for leadership? It starts with recognizing which friends fit into each category and then leaning on them when needed. Here are some scenarios to make you think about your own friends and how you could call on them when you need support, guidance or help as a leader.

1. BUILDER FRIEND

   Scenario: A leader is overwhelmed by a major project running late. Over drinks at the pub, they confide in their builder friend, who listens, encourages them not to give up and helps them brainstorm a plan to get back on track. The builder's faith and practical advice give the leader renewed energy and a clearer path forward.

2. NAVIGATOR FRIEND

   Scenario: The leader faces a tough decision about whether to let go of a struggling team member. He calls his navigator friend, who's known for wisdom and level-headed advice. The friend helps him weigh the pros and cons, consider the ethical implications and role-play the conversation, ensuring the leader acts with integrity and confidence.

3. ENERGIZER FRIEND

   Scenario: After a stressful week of back-to-back meetings and setbacks, the leader feels drained. He spends Saturday afternoon with his energizer friend, who makes him laugh and helps him unwind. This positive energy helps the leader return to work refreshed and ready to tackle challenges.

4. CONNECTOR FRIEND
Scenario: The leader's team needs a specialized consultant, but he doesn't know anyone in that field. He reaches out to his connector friend, who introduces him to a trusted expert. This connection saves time and brings valuable expertise to the project.

5. CHAMPION FRIEND
Scenario: The leader is doubting his ability after receiving tough feedback from his boss. His champion friend reminds him of his past successes, talks him up and helps him regain his self-confidence. This encouragement helps the leader bounce back and keep moving forward.

6. MIND OPENER FRIEND
Scenario: The leader is stuck in a rut, using the same old strategies. Over coffee, his mind opener friend challenges his assumptions and shares a new approach from a different industry. Inspired, the leader tries something new that improves his team's results.

7. COLLABORATOR FRIEND
Scenario: The leader is planning a big presentation and wants to rehearse. His collaborator friend, who shares similar interests, offers to listen, give feedback and help refine the message, making the final presentation much stronger.

8. COMPANION FRIEND
Scenario: The leader is facing burnout and questions whether leadership is worth it. His companion friend, who's always there in tough times, listens without judgment, offers emotional support, and reminds him of his values and purpose.

These examples show how a leader's personal friends, each playing a unique, vital role, can provide crucial outside help, perspective and energy, making it easier to manage professional challenges and lead with empathy and resilience.

A LEADER'S FRIENDSHIP TOOLKIT
In conclusion, the power of friendship extends far beyond shared laughter and good times: it is a foundational pillar for empathetic leadership. As Tom Rath's eight roles of friends illustrate, each friend brings a unique strength that can help leaders navigate the complexities of their professional journeys. Whether it's the unwavering encouragement of a Builder, the wise counsel of a Navigator or the infectious positivity of an Energizer, these relationships act as emotional anchors, helping leaders remain resilient, authentic, and grounded in their values.

Having the empathetic edge is about having the courage to seek support and inspiration from the people who know us best. Friends remind us that we're not alone in our struggles, offering perspective, comfort, and sometimes a much-needed push outside our comfort zones. They encourage us to view difficulties as possibilities and obstacles as building blocks for growth, fuelling our growth as leaders and as people.

Ultimately, friendships are not a distraction from leadership; they are the essential element that makes it sustainable and deeply human. By embracing the diverse roles our friends play in our lives, we become better equipped to lead with empathy, creativity and unwavering purpose. So, as you continue your leadership journey, remember to cherish and lean on your vital friends: they are your greatest allies in both work and life.

THE BIG QUESTIONS

1. Which of Tom Rath's eight friend roles (Builder, Champion, Companion, Connector, Collaborator, Energizer, Mind Opener, Navigator) do you already have in your life, and how have those friends helped you lead better?

2. When was the last time a friend gave you advice or support that changed your perspective or helped you through a tough spot at work?

3. How do you support others as a friend? Are you the Energizer, the Navigator, or maybe the Champion? How does that shape the way you lead?

4. How could you lean on your friends more intentionally to recharge, get advice, or gain fresh perspective when leadership gets tough?

> **Alone we can do so little; together we can do so much.**

Helen Keller

CHAPTER 13

THE POWER OF COLLECTIVE LEADERSHIP
WE

The 2025 golf's Ryder Cup wasn't just about golf. It was about leadership. Two captains. Two philosophies. And in the end, two very different outcomes.

From the first tee shot, the atmosphere was electric. Fans filled the grandstands, their cheers carrying across the course. Across Europe and the US, millions tuned in, bracing for the familiar drama of match play. But what played out over the week went beyond birdies and bogeys – it became a lesson in contrasting leadership styles, and in particular, the quiet strength of empathy.

On the European side, Luke Donald set a clear tone. His message? Togetherness. But more than that, he listened. He noticed when players needed encouragement and when they needed space. In press conferences and team meetings, he used inclusive language: *We've got each other's backs. We're ready as a group.* When reporters tried to spotlight individual stars, Donald redirected the credit to everyone, from caddies to assistants. He made sure every person in the camp felt seen and valued.

That empathy filtered through the team. Soon, Europe's players echoed it themselves, talking about "us," "our bond," and "the group." They weren't just teammates: they were a family.

The American camp took a different path. Their captain leaned into individuality and personal drive. His talks focused on perseverance and proving doubters wrong. Locker-room notes urged players to "bring your ego." For some, it sparked fire. But the focus stayed on personal battles, not collective strength. Empathy – the ability to tune into others' emotions and build trust – took a back seat. And as the pressure mounted, that absence became noticeable.

On the course, the contrast was striking. Europe stayed calm and connected. A clutch birdie or a comeback win was never celebrated as one player's moment – it was everyone's. Donald's refusal to claim credit gave his players more resolve, not less. They drew strength from each other because their leader had built that foundation of trust.

The Americans delivered flashes of brilliance, moments that lit up the crowd, but struggled to find consistency. Without the same sense of unity, momentum slipped away. The players looked like individuals carrying their own weight, rather than a team carrying each other.

When Europe lifted the trophy, it wasn't just about superior golf. It was a triumph of leadership rooted in empathy. By listening, by sharing credit, by making everyone feel part of something bigger, Donald created a culture where unity could thrive. The 2025 Ryder Cup proved it once again: in the highest-pressure moments, 'we' beats 'I.' And empathetic leadership is what makes 'we' possible.

WHY "WE HAVE" BEATS "I DID": THE CASE FOR EMPATHETIC LEADERSHIP

Imagine this scenario: you're sitting in a team meeting. The boss walks in, taps the table and says: *"I landed the big client. I redesigned the strategy. I managed the crisis."* Sounds confident, perhaps even impressive – briefly. But where does that leave the rest of the team? Nodding politely while checking their emails, wondering why they bothered staying late last week.

Now swap those words: *"We pulled late nights to close the deal. We figured out a clever workaround. We stuck together and got it done."* Suddenly, the room feels lighter. People sit up straighter. Smiles spread. Even the weekend hours don't sting so much. That's empathetic leadership at work, not just credit-sharing, but making people feel included, valued and genuinely seen.

EMPATHY IN EVERYDAY LEADERSHIP

The best leaders know this instinctively. They practise empathy not as a buzzword, but as a habit. Instead of claiming the spotlight, they spread it. Instead of pushing people, they tune into them. They know that teams don't thrive on fear or ego; they thrive when people feel safe, respected and part of something bigger.

Consider this: which teacher stuck with you – the one who bragged, *"I raised test scores,"* or the one who said, *"We made progress together this term"?* Which manager inspires more loyalty – the one who says, *"I made this project a success,"* or the one who thanks the group for pulling together under pressure?

Empathetic leadership builds trust, and trust builds resilience. When people feel valued, they tend to stay involved through difficulty, offering not just their time, but genuine commitment

WHY "WE" TEAMS WIN

Research shows that teams with empathetic leaders innovate more and stick together longer (see chapter 14). Why? Because empathy gives everyone a voice. When people feel heard, they're more likely to share bold ideas, the kind that rescue projects, win clients or spark growth.

And when setbacks hit (as they always do), "we" teams stand strong. They lean on one another, adjust together and recover faster.

Contrast that with 'I-first' leadership. Sure, it might deliver quick wins. A strong manager might step in and find a practical solution. But without empathy, teams burn out, grow cynical or quietly head for the door. Ego can grab a headline. Empathy builds a culture. And culture outlasts any one person.

LEADING WITH EMPATHY: HABITS THAT WORK

So, how do you lead with 'we' in mind? Here are some empathetic habits I've seen from great bosses, coaches and mentors – the kind that make teams want to stay late, not just because they have to, but because they want to:

- **Make team goals meaningful**: Don't just announce targets but invite everyone to define what success looks like together.

- **Celebrate achievements often**: A quick "Great job, team" with a spontaneous round of applause at the end of a meeting can mean more than an annual review.

- **Take the blame, share the credit**: Saying, "I should have noticed that" helps create trust. And acknowledging, "They did a fantastic job, we achieved it together" helps build loyalty.

- **Listen more than you talk**: Empathetic leaders don't dominate meetings; they create space for every voice to shape the path forward.

- **Ask for help**: "We need fresh ideas here" can unlock creative solutions and show that you value collaboration.

- **Build psychological safety**: Make it clear that questions aren't stupid, mistakes aren't fatal and wins, big or small, are worth celebrating together.

These aren't radical moves. They're small shifts in language and attitude. But they change the emotional climate of a workplace. They replace anxiety with trust, cynicism with pride, and detachment with engagement.

BRINGING IT BACK TO WORK

What happened on that golf course isn't just a sports story; it's a workplace story. Replace golfers with project managers, caddies with analysts, and fairways with office hallways, and the lesson is the same: empathy wins.

Empathetic leaders don't just manage; they connect. They don't just chase outcomes; they build cultures. They understand that success isn't a solo act; it's a shared journey. And they prove, again and again, that when you lead with 'we,' people will follow you through setbacks, long nights and high stakes.

So, the next time you step up in front of your team, whether you're pitching a client, steering a project or just opening Monday's staff meeting, think about the words you use. Are they "I closed, I built, I fixed"? Or are they "we created, we solved, we delivered"?

Because here's the not-so-secret truth: the pronouns you choose reveal how you lead. Too much 'I,' and you'll eventually find yourself leading alone. But lead with empathy, lead with 'we,' and you'll build something stronger: a team that not only wins but sticks around to celebrate together.

THE BIG QUESTIONS

1. When I talk about achievements with my team, am I using 'I' language or 'we' language? And how might that affect how people feel about their role in our success?

2. Do I actively listen to my team's needs and emotions, or am I too focused on driving results to notice when empathy is missing?

3. In moments of pressure, am I creating a culture where individuals feel safe to lean on each other, or one where everyone feels they have to go it alone?

4. When challenges arise, do I instinctively take the spotlight to solve them myself, or do I create space for the team to contribute and share ownership of the solution?

> **Empathy is one of our greatest tools of business that is most underused.**

Daniel Lubetzky

CHAPTER 14

LEADING WITH THE EMPATHETIC EDGE
A LEADERSHIP JOURNEY WORTH TAKING

THE EMPATHETIC EDGE

And here we are, at the end of this journey together. First of all, you've made it this far, congratulations! It means you've taken the time to explore what it truly means to lead with empathy, and that's no small achievement. This isn't just about reading a book, it's about reflecting, growing, and stepping into a version of leadership that's not only effective but also deeply human. But before we go any further, let's take a moment to breathe, smile and take stock of what we've covered.

Throughout this book, we've wandered through some pretty big ideas – self-worth, self-belief, self-awareness, individuality, optimism, mindset, perseverance, strengths, failure, luck, creativity, friendship and collective. Each of these traits is like a piece of a puzzle that comes together to form the picture of an empathetic leader. But let me tell you something: this isn't just about ticking off boxes. It's about weaving all these elements into the fabric of who you are as a person and as a leader.

Need more 'hard' evidence that this is good for business?

WHAT THE RESEARCH REALLY SAYS ABOUT EMPATHY

Let's cut through the buzzwords and management fads – empathy in leadership isn't just a feel-good idea; it's got serious science (and some pretty standout statistics) behind it. Years ago, people saw empathy as a 'soft skill,' but the research keeps piling up, showing it's anything but soft when it comes to results.

Here are a few key findings from recent studies that put all those old stereotypes to rest:

1. The Big Picture – 42 studies reviewed
   A giant review of academic research (we're talking 42 studies worldwide) spelled out just how far empathy goes in organizations. When leaders actually tune into their people, everything improves: trust shoots up, wellbeing gets a boost, performance climbs, and workplaces get fairer all around.

2. Empathy = High-Performing Leaders (across the globe)
   The Center for Creative Leadership looked at over 6,700 managers in 38 countries. Their findings: the more empathetic a leader was, the better their boss rated their performance. And it didn't matter if you were managing in Tokyo, Toronto or Turin; empathy worked everywhere.

3. Engagement – The Magic Number
   Research from Forbes and Catalyst found a dramatic "engagement gap." When leaders showed empathy, 76% of people reported feeling engaged at work. If empathy was lacking? That number plunged to just 32%.

4. Empathy Really Sparks Innovation
   As we explored in Chapter 11, if you want more creativity, it turns out empathy is the secret ingredient. Studies show that when leaders are empathetic, job satisfaction improves, and with that, everyday creativity takes off. People share their genuine ideas with you because they trust you'll listen rather than dismiss them out of hand.

5. Emotional Intelligence and Team Effectiveness
   Empathy sits at the core of emotional intelligence, but it's not just about feelings. When leaders practise it, there's less conflict, people work better together, and teams flat-out get more done. Dozens of studies now show that teams with empathetic leaders report higher productivity as well as better morale.

6. Retention, Loyalty and Wellbeing
   Want people to stick around? Turns out, empathy at the top is a major reason employees stay (or go). *Harvard Business Review* and others point out that empathy from leaders lowers burnout, ramps up loyalty and keeps workplace culture strong, even when things get tough.

Now that the science is clear, let's go back to what you can actually do with all this. If you've come this far, you know leading with empathy isn't just theory, it happens in the small, very human choices you make every single day. This is a good moment to step back and reflect on what we've covered so far, and talk about why these qualities matter so much and how they can give you that edge when leading a team.

SELF-WORTH: THE FOUNDATION OF IT ALL

Let's start with self-worth because honestly, it's the bedrock of everything else. If you don't believe deep down that you're worthy, worthy of respect, love, success or even just being heard, how can you possibly lead others with confidence? Self-worth isn't about arrogance or thinking you're better than anyone else; it's about knowing you have value just as you are.

An empathetic leader who understands their own worth doesn't need to prove themselves constantly or tear others down to feel bigger. Instead, they lift people up because they're secure in who they are. And let's be real: isn't that the kind of leader we all want to follow?

SELF-BELIEF: THE ROCKET FUEL

If self-worth is the foundation, then self-belief is the rocket fuel that propels you forward. It's that quiet voice inside reminding you, "You can handle this," even when things feel difficult or uncertain. Leadership isn't always smooth sailing, but believing in yourself is what keeps you steady when the waves start rocking the boat.

Empathetic leaders don't just believe in themselves; they inspire belief in others too. They see potential where others see problems, and possibilities where others see roadblocks. And that kind of belief? It's contagious.

SELF-AWARENESS: THE SPECIAL INGREDIENT

Self-awareness – the ability to look in the mirror and truly see yourself, flaws and all. It's not always easy or fun, but it's absolutely crucial for empathetic leadership. Why? Because if you don't understand your own emotions, triggers and blind spots, how can you possibly understand someone else's?

Self-awareness helps you navigate tricky situations with grace instead of reacting on autopilot. It allows you to step back and ask yourself questions like: "Why am I feeling this way?" or "How might my actions be affecting others?" And trust me, when your team sees that level of introspection in action, it sets the tone for open communication and mutual respect.

INDIVIDUALITY: THE GAME CHANGER

This is where individuality matters most – allowing yourself, and your team, to think differently and show up authentically.

It may feel a little uncomfortable at first, but it's worth it. When you and your team begin to embrace independent thinking, creativity and innovation tend to grow naturally.

OPTIMISM: THE LIGHT IN THE DARK

Now let me be clear: optimism doesn't mean walking around with rose-coloured glasses pretending everything is fine when it isn't. True optimism is about choosing to focus on possibilities rather than problems – it's about believing there's always a way forward, even when things feel impossible.

As an empathetic leader, your optimism becomes a guiding light for your team during tough times. It doesn't mean sugar-coating reality; it means saying, "Yes, this is hard but we'll get through it together." And let me tell you, those words can make all the difference.

MINDSET: YOUR LEADERSHIP GPS

Whether you realize it or not, your mindset shapes how you approach challenges, relationships and opportunities as a leader. A fixed mindset says, "This is just how things are," while a growth mindset says, "What can I learn from this?"

Empathetic leaders choose growth every time. They're not afraid to admit when they're wrong or when they don't have all the answers. Instead of seeing failure as the end of the road, they see it as a detour – a chance to recalibrate and try again. And honestly? That kind of resilience is inspiring.

PERSEVERANCE: THE GLUE THAT HOLDS IT ALL TOGETHER

If leadership were easy, everyone would do it but we all know that's not the case. Perseverance is what keeps you going when things get tough. It's about showing up day after day, even when progress feels slow or invisible, and trusting that your efforts will pay off.

Empathetic leaders don't give up on themselves, or their teams, when times get hard. They dig deep into their reserves of resilience and determination because they know leadership isn't about perfection; it's about persistence.

STRENGTHS: WHAT COMES NATURALLY TO YOU

Strengths sit at the heart of effective leadership, yet they are often overlooked. Too often, people focus on their weaknesses instead of recognizing what they naturally do well.

Empathetic leaders know their strengths inside out and they use them unapologetically. But more importantly? They help others discover their strengths too. They create environments where people feel seen for who they are and valued for what they bring to the table.

FAILURE: YOUR UNLIKELY ALLY

Failure can be uncomfortable to think about, but it plays an important role in growth. It isn't the enemy of good leadership; in many ways, it's a quiet teacher. Mistakes will happen. You'll misjudge situations, take wrong turns or fall short at times, and that's part of the process.

In fact, it's necessary. Failure is where real growth happens. It's where you learn what doesn't work, where you build resilience and figure out how to bounce back stronger. Empathetic leaders don't fear failure; they own it, learn from it and use those lessons to grow. And when your team sees you handle failure with grace, they'll feel safe to take risks and innovate too. Because here's the secret: failure isn't the opposite of success – it's just a step on the way there.

LUCK – WHEN PREPARATION MEETS OPPORTUNITY

Feeling lucky? From small superstitions to chance moments, luck can add an extra layer of empathy. Luck tends to appear unexpectedly, often disguised as coincidence or timing!

Stay ready for those offbeat chats, strange coincidences or surprise emails. Stay curious and open to whatever comes your way because you never know what might be waiting just around the corner!

CREATIVITY: YOUR ROCKET BOOSTER

Take a minute to really check out your workspace. Does it have that spark, that energy that gets creativity flowing? If not, maybe it's time to mix things up! A creative and energizing atmosphere can consistently strengthen team performance.

Creative leaders don't just challenge convention – they rethink it entirely. They're all about fresh ideas and aren't stuck on 'how it's always been done.' When you create a space that welcomes new thinking, you open the door to real innovation and exciting results.

FRIENDSHIP: YOUR SUPPORT NETWORK

You might call them friends, mates or your pals, but whatever the name, these people play an important role in helping you build empathy. It's reassuring to know you have eight different types of friends to support you through challenges and celebrate the good moments, the tough stuff and cheer you on when things get exciting.

So don't let those "I'm a fraud" or "I don't belong here" thoughts stop you from reaching out. Your friends know you inside out, so go ahead and ask for their help and advice. That's what friends are for!

"WE" NOT "I":
THE HEART OF TRUE LEADERSHIP

At its heart, "we not I" is about more than grammar – it's about empathy. Leaders who use 'we' show they see and value the people around them. Instead of grabbing credit, they share it. Instead of demanding loyalty, they earn it. This isn't false modesty; it's about trust.

When teams feel their leader genuinely cares, they bring their best. Empathetic leadership turns groups into real teams by shifting the focus from ego to collective success.

BRINGING IT ALL TOGETHER

So where does this leave us? In many ways, right back where we began – with you. Because at its core, empathetic leadership isn't about following a rigid formula or ticking off a checklist. It's about showing up as yourself, consistently and with intention.

It's about leading with care rather than ego; listening more than speaking; lifting others up rather than pulling them down; owning mistakes instead of defending them; and choosing kindness, even when it isn't the easiest option.

It's about being human and allowing others to be human too.

That said, empathy doesn't mean lowering expectations. There will still be moments that call for clarity, boundaries and difficult decisions. Leading with empathy means handling those moments calmly, fairly and with respect.

It won't always be easy. Few worthwhile things are. But leading this way has lasting impact, not just on your team, but on you as well. Because in the end, people won't remember how many targets you met or meetings you ran. They'll remember how you made them feel.

So move forward with empathy at the centre of how you lead in a way that feels genuine to you.

> I've learned that people will forget what you said, people will forget what you did, but people will never forget how you made them feel.

Maya Angelou

REFERENCES AND RESOURCES

KICK OFF
Jacob Rees-Mogg. https://www.bbc.co.uk/news/uk-politics-61522973

CHAPTER 1
"Our Founder." *Value of the Person*. https://www.valueoftheperson.com/about-us/our-founder/

Dr Ali Binazi. "Are You a Miracle?" *HuffPost*, June 2011. https://bit.ly/2tPjKzm

CHAPTER 2
Terry Gross. "Tom Hanks Says Self-Doubt Is 'A High-Wire Act That We All Walk.'" *National Public Radio*, 26 April 2016. https://n.pr/2GpzHPs

Dr Valerie Young. "The 5 Types of Imposters." *Imposter Syndrome Institute*, 2019. https://impostorsyndrome.com/

CHAPTER 3
Rod Judkins. *Change your Mind*. Richmond, Australia: Hardie Grant, 2013

Joseph Luft and Harrington Ingham. "The Johari Window: a graphic model of interpersonal awareness." Proceedings of the Western Training Laboratory in Group Development, University of California, Los Angeles, 1955

Charles Handy. *21 Ideas for Managers*. San Francisco: Jossey-Bass, 2000

Loretta Malandro. *Fearless Leadership*. New York: McGraw-Hill Education, 2009

CHAPTER 4

Rob Siltanen. "The Real Story Behind Apple's 'Think Different' Campaign." *Forbes*, 14 December 2011. https://bit.ly/37xPeJ6

Phillip Zimbardo. "Stanford Prison Experiment." *Social Psychology Network*, 1971. https://bit.ly/3aGRvn9

CHAPTER 5

Seph Fontane Pennock. "Who is Martin Seligman and what does he do?" *Positive Psychology Program*, 13 March 2017, available at: https://bit.ly/2dj8phU

CHAPTER 6

Bill Gates. *Business @ the Speed of Thought: Succeeding in the Digital Economy*. Grand Central Publishing, 1999

Bill Gates. "The Internet Tidal Wave." memo, 26 May 1995, available at: https://bit.ly/1CUujZJ

Carol Dweck. *Mindset: The New Psychology of Success*. Ballantine Books, updated edition, 2007

CHAPTER 8

Gallup, StrengthsFinder (now CliftonStrengths), available at: www.gallupstrengthscenter.com

VIA Character Strengths, available at: www.viacharacter.org

Sally Bibb. *The Strengths Book*. LID Publishing, 2017

Tom Rath and Gallup, StrengthsFinder 2.0, Gallup Press, 2007

CHAPTER 10

Marguerite Ward. "Mark Zuckerberg Returns to the Harvard Dorm Room Where Facebook Was Born." *CNBC*. 25 May 2017. https://www.cnbc.com/2017/05/25/mark-zuckerberg-returns-to-the-harvard-dorm-wherefacebook-was-born.html

CHAPTER 11

Colette Martin and Kristi Hedges. "Creativity is the new black." *Forbes*, 16 July 2010. https://www.forbes.com/sites/work-in-progress/2010/07/16/creativity-is-the-new-black/?sh=42169eaa62df

Pilita Clark. "How the modern office is killing our creativity." *Financial Times*, 15 March 2019. https://www.ft.com/content/6148ec14-457a-11e9-a965-23d669740bfb

CHAPTER 12

Tom Rath. *Vital Friends: The People You Can't Afford to Live Without*. Washington, DC: Gallup Press, 2006

CHAPTER 14

Springer, Systematic Review, 2025

Center for Creative Leadership, Global Empathy Study

Forbes/Catalyct, 2023

Kock et al., 2018 (PMC, Emotional Intelligence Studies)

Harvard Business Review, 2023

ABOUT THE AUTHOR

NEIL FRANCIS is a leadership advisor, author and entrepreneur based in Scotland.

He works with CEOs, senior leaders, charity leaders and entrepreneurs, supporting them to build resilient, people-centred organizations where performance and empathy go hand in hand.

He is the author of *The Creative Thinking Book*, *Inspired Thinking*, *Positive Thinking*, *The Entrepreneur's Book* and *Changing Course*. His work has been translated into multiple languages, including Chinese, and is widely used by leaders seeking clarity, perspective and more human approaches to leadership.

In 2006, at the age of 41, Neil suffered a life-changing stroke – an experience that fundamentally reshaped his understanding of leadership, identity and success. Since then, his work has focused on helping leaders navigate challenge, uncertainty and change with clarity, emotional intelligence and humanity.

Alongside his advisory work and writing, Neil has spent more than 30 years as an entrepreneur, founding, growing and exiting digital and technology businesses. This real-world experience continues to inform his leadership perspective, grounding his work in the realities of decision-making, responsibility and organizational life.

www.neil-francis.com
neil@neil-francis.com

BY THE SAME AUTHOR

£9.99/$14.95
ISBN:978-1-915951-25-0

£9.99/$14.95
ISBN: 978-1-911671-44-2

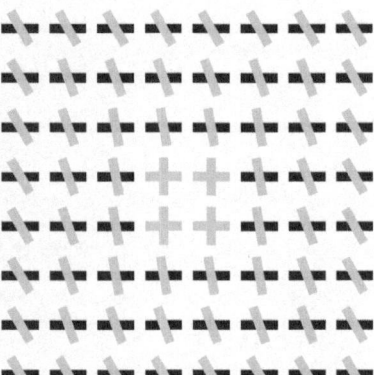

£9.99/$14.95
ISBN: 978-1-912555-15-4

£9.99/$14.95
ISBN: 978-1-912555-77-2